FIND OUT ABOUT RICKY'S FAVES!

His favorite movie: *The Godfather*

His favorite kind of food: **Cuban**

His favorite designer: **Giorgio Armani**

His favorite type of music: **Classical**

His favorite vacation spot: **Puerto Rico**

AND MUCH MORE!

RICKY MARTIN

Elina Furman

St. Martin's Paperbacks

RICKY MARTIN

Copyright © 1999 by Elina Furman.

Cover photograph © Barry King /Shooting Star.

ISBN: 0-312-97322-5

Printed in the United States of America

St. Martin's Paperbacks edition/June 1999

10 9 8 7 6 5 4 3 2

For My Grandmother, Eteri

Acknowledgments

I'd **like to** thank everyone who helped me put this book together, including my editor, Glenda Howard, for all her effort and dedication, and my agent, Giles Anderson, who played an instrumental role in bringing this project to fruition. As always, my mother, Mira, for her support and encouragement. And none of this could have been possible without my sister Leah's input and meticulous attention to detail. Finally, I would like to thank John Nikkah for his invaluable research assistance.

Contents

INTRODUCTION

Blazing a Path to Glory

Go! Go! Go! Before it was his claim to fame, the phrase was Ricky Martin's heartfelt motto. Ever since his early years as a sprightly member of Menudo, the world's longest running boy band, Ricky was on the fast track. With countless sold-out concerts, two multiplatinum albums, a Grammy Award for Best Latin Pop Performance, and triumphant stints on Broadway and U.S. television, Ricky Martin is a certified international darling, boasting fans in every corner of the globe— from Asia to Europe to the United States.

Born Enrique Martin Morales in San Jose, Puerto Rico, on December 24, 1971, Ricky first caught the public's eye as one of the more talented members of Menudo. In 1989, he returned to Puerto Rico to complete his education, choosing to pursue an acting career by taking on roles in the musical *Mama Ama El Rock* and the highly rated Mexican daytime drama, *Alcanzar Una Estrealla II*. Earning his first Heraldo, Mexico's equivalent of the Academy Award, for the series' film spin-off, Ricky was poised on the brink of greatness.

The decision to go back to his first love, singing and composing, resulted in the release of his self-titled debut. But it wasn't until his second solo effort, *Me*

Amaras, that Ricky was finally catapulted to the pantheon of Latino music. Going platinum in many countries, the album skyrocketed to the top of the Latin charts, earning him a well-deserved Billboard New Latin Artist award in 1993.

As if to prove that he had only just begun to win, Ricky Martin returned to acting in the long-running American television drama, *General Hospital*. In 1994 he became a regular cast member, playing a part that was close to his heart. As Miguel, a former pop star from Puerto Rico, Ricky was able to showcase his vocal talents. This opportunity was what finally earned him a leading role in the Broadway production of *Les Miserables*.

In the midst of this exciting experience, a third recording, titled *A Medio Vivir*, was unveiled to the world. The album's maturity and artistic virtuosity transformed Ricky into an international superstar known for his entrancing performances and electrifying stage presence. The five million copies sold is a true testament to Ricky Martin's domination of the Latin music market.

His subsequent album, *Vuelve*, was followed by unprecedented critical and commercial success, as well as a worldwide tour to end all tours. As the proud owner of a Grammy for this widely praised contribution, he is staying true to his motto by going all the way to an English crossover. Having managed to stun even the blasé audience of music industry insiders with his high-octane performance at the 1999 Grammy Awards, his two latest albums, *Vuelve* and the English *Ricky Martin*, have attracted new fans by the millions. Simultaneously navigating the Spanish- and English-speaking territories at the tender age of twenty-eight, Ricky Martin has proven that he will continue to break through cultural and artistic boundaries for many years to come.

CHAPTER 1

Child of Puerto Rico

San Juan, a town nestled deep within the ruggedly landscaped island of Puerto Rico, was and continues to be a place Ricky Martin is proud to call home. As the capital of Puerto Rico, San Juan (population 1.5 million) enjoys a comfortable blend of Old World tradition and contemporary mores. As one of the city's 1.3 million Roman Catholics, Ricky Martin has come to embody everything that's good about the Puerto Rican people: their ample pride, intense spirituality, and burning passion for dance and music.

Although it is governed by the policies of the U.S. and is considered a U.S. territory, Puerto Rico has held on to its diverse cultural heritage. Intermingling Spanish, African, and Taino traditions, Puerto Rico's cultural backdrop is anything but homogenous. While Spanish is still the main language, American and Amerindian words are sprinkled liberally within the local patois. As for the country's salt-of-the-earth citizens, while they may pray on Catholic altars, they are even more fiercely aligned to homespun spiritualism and folkloric beliefs.

Traveling through Puerto Rico's regions, one can see the impact of commercialization. More noticeable, however, are the expansive colonial towns that resonate with the domestic tranquility of bygone eras. Nestled between Hispaniola and the archipelagoes of the Leeward Islands, Puerto Rico owes a great deal of its demographic beauty to the rocky foothills of Cordillera Central, and its cultural splendor can be traced back to the early Spanish settlers.

During the 1970s, San Juan was an explosive mecca of activity, sound, pulsating rhythms, and color. It was a joyful time, when televisions became mainstream, employment opportunities were plentiful, and "salsa" was heard on every street corner. A simpler and more innocent decade, the seventies were permeated with an aura of celebration and optimism.

San Juan sowed the seeds that would later blossom into the international superstar known to millions as Ricky Martin. "That young child is still alive," Ricky reflected, "and he has transformed himself into the judge of the man that I have become."

Born on December 24, 1971, to Nereida Morales and Enrique Martin Negroni, Ricky Martin was the first and only son of the marriage. As the couple's sole child, Ricky enjoyed the unconditional affection, support, and attention of the family; the kind of love that nurtures greatness; the kind of support that would eventually imbue him with the confidence and charisma needed to dazzle mammoth crowds in every corner of the globe.

As a member of a middle class family—his father was a psychologist and his mother an accountant—Ricky's early childhood could be described in three simple words: carefree, joyful, and uninhibited. Even when his parents announced that a divorce was imminent on the horizon, Ricky was spared the trauma of a sudden separation. The love of his family sheltered the two-year-old from having to witness any fights or conflicts on the family front. For all Ricky knew, his family unit was as tightly knit as ever.

Sadly, that blissful ignorance would not last forever. When petitioning for a divorce, Ricky's mother and father asked him the impossible—to choose whom he would live with. Ricky spent endless hours in deliberation, deciding, in the end, that he loved both parents too much to part from either of them. Thanks to his parents' wisdom, he never had to pick a favorite. They finally agreed that sharing custody would be in their son's best interest. "It was really hard for my parents because when they got a divorce, they fought over who would be my legal guardian," he recounted to *Salut*. "And it's hard for a child to choose between his mother and father."

Being shepherded from home to home, Ricky savored the variety that his ever-changing settings afforded him, a variety that would later manifest itself in his constant need to be on the move and spread his music throughout the world. Young Ricky appreciated his parents' effort to part on friendly terms. At that point in his life, Nereida and Enrique were very receptive to his wishes, allowing him the freedom to come and go as he pleased. "My childhood was very healthy, near to my parents, who were divorced," Ricky confirmed. "I did whatever I wanted; I lived with my mother, if I wanted to be with her; and with my father in the same way. I had the same affection from both of them."

While most kids his age would be adversely affected by a family's disintegration, Ricky wasn't at all bothered by the new circumstance. Upon realizing what he stood to gain from the arrangement, any initial discomfort or worry he may have felt quickly faded into the background. Already a wheeler and dealer, Ricky managed to find a way to take advantage of the divorce by playing on the guilt of his newly single and unsuspecting parents. No matter what he wanted, whether it would a new toy or time off to play with his friends, his parents made sure that Ricky wasn't disappointed. He boasted to *Salut*, "It was actually in my favor that they had broken up: they dedicated themselves entirely to me, and I made them do whatever I wanted them to do!"

When the dust of the divorce settled, Ricky was free to live the carefree existence of an average kid. As a student at a Catholic school located only a block from his house, he preferred to spend his days riding his bike, getting into trouble with the neighborhood kids, and playing music in his room. From an early age, Ricky was a natural leader. He was extremely social, the type of kid whom everyone is drawn to and wants to befriend. As with many things that come too easily, Ricky took his friendships for granted, assuming that everyone was as popular as he was.

One of his favorite childhood pastimes also included visiting his grandmother, Iraida, who taught him the importance of fighting for his beliefs and the necessity of self-expression. It was she who also gave him the nickname "Kiki," used to this day by his family and close friends. An artist in her own right, Iraida also invested Ricky with his love for painting and writing. While preparing dinner or relaxing in the house, the two would have long conversations about art and literature. She would also weave richly detailed tales about his ancestors and heritage. Ricky remembers those times as some of the most pleasant in his life. "I'm totally in love with my grandmother," he told

Star Club. "She is the one person I'm closest to in the whole world. I have to admit that I've spent more time with her than with my own mother. It's a bit like she brought me up and taught me the things in life. She made me believe in me since the beginning."

Enjoying a close relationship with his grandmother didn't stop Ricky from forming a strong bond to his mother. Working all day, every day to support her family, Nereida Morales tried to devote as much time to Ricky as possible. Alas, the demands of her career were great, and she often relied on Ricky's grandmother to fill the gaps. She did, however, make up for whatever time the two had lost by showering her young son with extra affection. "As soon as she sees me, she's always after me," Ricky told *Star Club.* "She kisses me and treats me like a king! It can seem stupid but I really appreciate the unconditional love she gives me."

Judging by the amount of attention lavished upon the youngster, it's not difficult to guess where his exhibitionist tendencies came from. A typical only child, he couldn't get enough of the spotlight, craving more and more focus as the years progressed. Besides winning a baby beauty contest as an infant, he was an active participant in church choirs and school plays. For Ricky, being onstage was synonymous with being loved. It was like having an even bigger family to adore and admire his every move and gesture.

Television also played a vital role in spawning his affinity for becoming a media darling. In the 1970s, every middle class family could afford a television, and Ricky's was no exception. He was captivated with the images on the small screen, spending countless hours flipping through the channels. But Ricky could never be satisfied in simply watching other people live out their dreams. He wanted a piece of the action for himself, and vowed to one day make his own mark as a performer.

Suffering as he was from the only-child syndrome, Ricky was due for a wake-up call. He got exactly that when both his parents remarried. He wasn't so much disturbed by his step-parents as the fact that he would have five new brothers and sisters usurping his throne. Eventually, the competitive sibling rivalry would subside, with Ricky forming important attachments to all of his five brother and sisters, Fernando, Angel, Eric, Daniel, and Vanessa. "My familiar life is very calm and my family is very united," he expressed to *Jet-Set*. "I have five brothers and sisters, two of my mother's part and three of my father's part."

Losing the attention he desperately craved from his family, Ricky spent his time daydreaming about becoming a huge superstar, with millions of fans falling at his feet. The idea of worldwide fame, recognition, and big dollars permanently emblazoned itself upon the boy's young mind. He would forever pursue his quest for stardom, or die trying.

Although television was responsible for piquing Ricky's interest in the entertainment industry, music, not acting, was his true dream. While he had never trained formally, he was born with an innate sense of rhythm and pitch. "As you know Puerto Ricans are very musical people," explained Ricky. "They say that babies are born with a sense of rhythm in Puerto Rico. Music is a part of life there. There's no school where you can go and learn it. It's just a question of feeling it."

At the tender age of six, Ricky didn't know what he was going to do. In a manner befitting his age, he really didn't care what he did so long as everyone knew his name. "I was rather a fickle-minded youngster, footloose and fancy free. I wanted to do so many things," he told *The Hindustan Times*. Of course, no one could expect him to find his life's purpose so early in his career. He would have many years to figure that out.

In the meanwhile, Ricky had worked hard at getting all the gestures and facial expressions of commercial actors down pat. All that was left to do now was convince his parents to take time out of their busy schedules and act as chaperones during the busy commercial circuit. As he feared that his mother would react adversely to his proposition of entering show business, Ricky first popped the question to his dad. Much to his surprise, his father not only accepted the idea, he also offered to help Ricky realize his dream. His mother also came around when she discovered how talented and ambitious her son had become.

"When I was six, I said to my dad, 'Dad, I want to be an artist!' Well, he didn't know what hit him, of course," Ricky told *Hitkrant*. " 'Where did you get that idea?' But he also said, 'If you want to become an artist, how can we get you there?' But my dad is a psychologist and my mom is an accountant; they don't have anything to do with show business. They wanted to give their son everything he wanted, so they immediately thought: how can we help? 'No problem, I'll handle it,' I said, as opinionated six-year-olds do. My dad took me to a modeling agency and at age seven I did my first commercial for TV and I kept doing that for a while."

Ricky was a natural in front of the camera, or so the casting directors and agents kept telling him. More important, Ricky's skills were evidenced by his success in booking one commercial after another. His Kewpie doll looks and charming smile had the power to open even the most exclusive of doors. And once he was in, Ricky was impossible to resist. His first commercial was for a soda campaign, and he enjoyed the experience thoroughly. So much so, in fact, that it was only a matter of time until he became one of the most sought-after young actors. Landing a myriad of roles in television ads, he enjoyed being pampered and fussed over by the hairstylists and makeup artists. Feeling special had always come easy for the extroverted youngster, but the more affection he received, the more he craved it. Ricky was all about extremes; too much love was simply never enough.

Even as he was gaining immense accolades from casting directors all over town, Ricky started searching for something more. His quest for the good life led him to seek counsel from a fortune-teller. He was only seven years old, but he knew exactly what he wanted to hear. When the "witch," as he calls her, read his fate, she informed the young boy that he would one day grow up to become a famous artist. Ricky was forever haunted by the memory of that event. He was now convinced that total world domination would only be a matter of time. As luck should have it, the fortune-teller was right. "Even this witch had something to do with it, with me wanting to affect people in a positive way when it comes to music," he told the *Union-Tribune*.

He was now anxious to begin what he thought would be a new life, filled with endless glamour and excitement. Every minute he waited seemed like an eternity. While most of his classmates were too busy playing kick-the-can in the San Juan streets to give their future much thought, Ricky was looking toward a greater destiny.

Because he was very close to his family, he shared his hopes with his parents, grandma, and anyone else who would listen. He would bend their weary ears for hours, describing the places he would visit, the ample hotel suites he would occupy, and the many fans that would adore him. This activity was a regular event in the close-knit household. "I saw myself singing in different countries," he explained to *Diversion*.

Ricky's drive to become the best forced his parents to take notice, and they enrolled him in acting and singing courses. Good looks and natural talent were all well and good, but if he was really going to be a big star, he would need all the help he could get. Of course, he had to promise that his schoolwork wouldn't suffer in the meantime. Living within a family of professionals, Ricky was taught to value education from an early age. Balancing his busy school life with his artistic training, the young boy showed his parents that he could accomplish anything he set his mind to.

Gaining wide exposure to the world of show business through television, he soon realized his life's ambition. At the time, a boy band going under the title Menudo had been taking the world by storm. They were touring the country, giving interviews, and making appearances on television. Watching the group's show-stopping performances and reading about them in the newspapers was a bittersweet enterprise. On the one hand, he was proud of the Latin boys' success and domination of the pop charts. On the other, he coveted their fame and badly wanted to become a member.

What began as a simple idea soon escalated into a full-blown obsession with everything Menudo. "Well, at that time there was a boy group, Menudo, in South America and they were very successful," Ricky told *Hitkrant*. "That became my next project: how can I get into that group? I read an interview with those guys and they said, 'If you want to join the group you have to come to the management's office, fill out an application form. They'll call you and tell you if they're interested or not.' "

Perhaps not surprisingly, artistry had very little to do with drawing young Ricky to Menudo. At that point of his life, he cared very little about honing his craft or spreading his message of cultural tolerance and diversity. Singing was just a means to an end, and the end had everything to do with meeting girls and living the fast life of a rock star. "I didn't want to be a singer. What I wanted was to be in Menudo," said Ricky. "I wanted to give concerts, to travel, to meet the pretty girls. I had been a fan of the group since it began in 1977. I was always stubbornly determined to be one of them."

He even began beefing up the time he spent on singing and dancing lessons. When the opportunity to try out for the group presented itself, he wanted to be ready. His small size, however, seemed to be an obstacle. Although he was short, Ricky believed that he could become taller if he tried. That's how determined he was to become a member.

To achieve his goal, Ricky initiated a rigorous physical training regime. "I told my parents, 'When I'm older, I want to be a Menudo!' That Puerto Rican group, made of five boys aged from twelve to sixteen, got started in 1976 and has been the first of all boy bands," he revealed to *Salut*. "Those boys were like a dream because they were singing, dancing, traveling all over the world, and getting to meet lots of girls! And so, between the ages of six and twelve, I prepared myself to become a Menudo. I even started to play basketball to grow faster!''

Nothing was going to sway Ricky from the path he had chosen to pursue. His parents were aware of his desire to go on tour with the group, but dismissed it as just another one of his many half-baked ideas. He was always coming up with some new plan to become successful. From the time he was six years old, he was like a musical entrepreneur generating get-rich-quick schemes. So when Ricky informed them of his plan to enter the esteemed Menudo ranks, they never believed that he would one day make good on his promise.

For years, Ricky ate, slept, and dreamed Menudo. Even his closest friends grew tired of listening to him rattle on about all the fun he was going to have traversing the globe. Much like his parents, they didn't take Ricky's agenda too seriously, choosing to humor him instead. While his plans were met with skepticism from all camps, it was his grandmother that encouraged him to hold tight to his dream. Not for one minute did she doubt his ability to become a part of Menudo. She had firsthand knowledge of Ricky's will power, and was confident that he would indeed be invited to join the group.

Of course, there *was* the not-so-small matter of an audition to get through. No stranger to making a good impression, Ricky had learned all about auditioning from his days in commercials. He was a pro at smiling on cue, looking sad if need be, or feigning enthusiasm. Of course, when it came to Menudo, he wouldn't have to pretend to be excited. He had been waiting for this day for quite some time.

As soon as he turned twelve years old and became

eligible, Ricky was optimistic that this would be his year; the year that the fortune-teller's sweet prediction would come to pass. The search for the newest Menudo had begun. Ricky Melendez had quit the group, leaving a space open for a new recruit. If ever fate seemed to be on his side, it was now. Not only did he turn twelve years old right around the time a spot opened in the group, he and his predecessor shared the same first name.

Before he could claim his post as the youngest member of Menudo, Ricky would have to fill out a form and wait for the group's manager, Edgardo Diaz, to extend an invitation. To his dismay, Ricky never got the call he waited for. While he had all the credentials needed to join Menudo—good looks, a great singing voice, dancing ability—Diaz worried that the young boy's diminutive stature would imbalance the rest of the group's lofty proportions. Ricky was crushed by the disheartening news. He had suspected that his height would interfere, but always hoped that the manager would overlook this minor flaw. Now, he would have to say goodbye to his lifelong dream. Or would he?

Anyone else would have given the dream up for dead, but not Ricky. Instead of viewing the rejection as the final word, he saw it as a mere delay. He was now even more determined to get selected. Nothing would stop him.

Meanwhile, destiny was playing out her own hand. The Menudo managerial team had scoured the countryside looking for a replacement, but wherever they went they couldn't find the person who had that unique combination of brains, looks, and talent. After two years of fruitless searching, they were no closer to finding an adequate substitute. ''The first two times I auditioned, they told me no, that I was too little. Ricky Melendez left, and I was one of the ones hoping to replace him,'' explained Ricky. ''They searched for his replacement for two years, until finally they gave me a third audition.''

Before setting out for the audition, Ricky didn't want to get his family's hopes up too high, electing to secretly transport himself by bicycle. He was all anticipation and anxiety. Would this be the moment he had been waiting for, or was he just setting himself up for another disappointment? This question raced through his mind as he sped on his bike to the audition. When he entered the room, the height issue was still paramount in everyone's mind. But this time, Diaz was willing to suspend his skepticism long enough for Ricky to showcase his talents. ''[The manager] didn't want me because I was too small,'' he conveyed to *Star Club*. ''He said no to me three times in a year, until the day when he accepted me. He tested me to see how well I could sing, dance, and play to even out my height. It was frustrating.''

Ricky had been waiting for this moment for as long as he could remember. The pressure, however, had very little effect on him. Taking full advantage of this once-in-a-lifetime opportunity, he succeeded in impressing the previously recalcitrant man. As he wound down his routine, Ricky could immediately gauge the impression he had made. Diaz nodded approvingly, and wasted no time informing Ricky that he would be the newest member of the Menudo family. The last time proved to be the charm, and he rejoiced at the fact that all of his hard work, dedication, and persistence had finally paid off.

Riding faster than the speed of light, Ricky pedaled home to break the phenomenal news. So elated was he

at having fulfilled his deepest desires that he completely forgot about the effect that his long-term separation would have on the family. His parents had never
thought Ricky would get so far. They didn't even know
where he had been all day. When he stormed into his
house, he was so breathless with joy that he could hardly string two sentences together. Through mumbled
words and many fits and starts, his family finally made
out what had happened. Ricky would be leaving home
to join Menudo on the road. As soon as the initial shock
wore off, his family expressed a mixed reaction to the
news. "My parents were very supportive, but they
weren't the typical stage parents," he said during an
America Online chat. "I came back home, telling my
parents that I was leaving to be an entertainer. I was
twelve years old at the time. They started laughing and
then they started crying. This was twelve years ago."

Their baby was, after all, only twelve years old.
How would he manage to live on his own? Who
would take care of him? Would he be able to get
through the tough training program exacted by Menudo's managerial team? Ricky's parents were rightly
concerned about his welfare. Not yet a teenager, he
would be exposed to some of the most unsavory elements of show business.

Since both parents prided themselves on raising their
son as a God-fearing Catholic, the idea of his joining
the internationally renowned group sat none too well
with them. Of course, they couldn't have known that
the concerns they had with the music lifestyle were
exactly what drew Ricky to the group. He was way
ahead of his time, and wanted to meet as many girls
and have as much fun as possible. He loved the idea
of hanging out with a group of older guys.The allure

of finally becoming a man was just too great, and Ricky wasted no time pouting, stamping his feet, and persuading his family to approve the idea. "My parents were terrified, because that meant I had to leave for Orlando, Florida, where the group was based," Ricky told *Salut*. "But I was so happy. My parents finally accepted, because they knew that was my dream, and they signed the deal with tears in their eyes."

After a lengthy conference with group manager Diaz, Ricky's parents agreed to the proposition, but not before they got the manager's word that Ricky would be well taken care of and shielded from some of the more R-rated facets of pandemonium. It was impossible to resist Ricky's arguments. He had thought of little else for years, and would not let his parents' love and concern deter him from his course. He was a man with a mission if ever there was one.

As soon as the deal was finalized, Ricky's parents wept over the loss of their son. Not only were they a little apprehensive, they were also legitimately hurt. Instead of perceiving his elation as a desire to join the group, they believed that it was a sign that he wasn't happy with his family life. Ricky had always been so close to them, they never for once suspected that leaving the family fold would be so seductive. But as loving parents, they put their selfish feelings aside, choosing to focus instead on the joy and happiness written all over Ricky's beaming face. "I was so enthusiastic about being part of the group that even my parents were surprised about how easily I could distance myself from them," he said. "It seemed unreal to them that a child who was so mild-mannered, and loved being home so much, could leave without any regrets."

*   *   *

The several weeks of anticipation Ricky had to endure before departing for Orlando were spent sailing on cloud nine. The majority of his time went on pondering his glorious fate. He could hardly believe what was happening to him. When he first made it into the group, all he had thought about was convincing his parents to give him their blessing. Now, he was free to fantasize about the exciting new chapter in his life. To that end, the young boy with stars in his eyes daydreamed about America. Having heard many stories about the "land of opportunity," Ricky was anxious to stake his claim on the new frontier. He knew just enough English to communicate with the locals, and looked forward to visiting Disney World and shopping centers. Although he shared a strong connection with his homeland, the lure of America was impossible to resist.

While the luminous future took precedence in Ricky's mind, the last few weeks with his family were still some of the most bittersweet he had known. It was July, 1984, and Ricky was actually scared to leave home. Since his tranquil family atmosphere had shielded him from having to deal with any problems, he fretted about being able to cope with life's many difficulties. Ricky was also concerned about getting homesick. The Menudo schedule was so exacting, he would probably have little time for visits. In the end, however, his desire for fame and celebrity won out. But his feelings of joy presented another problem. He didn't want to insult his family by acting too thrilled at the prospect of flying the coop. While his parents were walking around looking dour, it took all of Ricky's will power to curb his vivacity.

When the day came to say *adios*, there wasn't a single dry eye in the house. Although the family had organized a small, informal farewell party, the shindig seemed more like a funeral than a celebration. After receiving his parting gifts and all the kisses and hugs he could stand, Ricky made his way for the door. His vision was fixed on the future, and it seemed that he was forever lost to his family. But as his feet moved briskly toward an unknown world, he turned hesitantly around one last time. Rushing back into his family's loving arms for one last hug, he appeared to be saying that there would be no real goodbyes that day. Ricky would remain a child of Puerto Rico until the end of time.

CHAPTER 2

Menudo Mania

On July 10, 1984, Ricky was initiated as Menudo's newest member. But contrary to what most of Ricky Martin's fans believe, Menudo was popular long before little Ricky came on board. Of course, his presence made for an exciting addition to the team, but it was not solely responsible for Menudo's worldwide success.

It was in 1977 that Edgardo Diaz brainstormed the brilliant musical concept that would later bear the widely recognized Menudo title. Diaz conceived a musical group that would remain forever young, not only in people's hearts, but in their eyes as well. How he planned to accomplish this task was by simply upgrading each member on their seventeenth birthday to a younger model. That way, the music would remain fresh and the profits consistent. Boys and girls from all backgrounds would keep tuning in, and like their idols, would pass the Menudo legacy on to their young successors.

The idea may have been sound, but its execution would decide whether Menudo would triumph or fizzle. The inaugural group would first have to be assembled. Holding open auditions for Latino teenage boys, Diaz had to sift through thousands of applications and sit through thousands of murdered melodies to find his first batch of Menudoans, including brothers Carlos, Oscar, and Ricky Melendez and Nefty and Fernando Sallaberry. Then he had to train them, hiring vocal coaches and dance instructors to show them the ropes. From there, it was on to the studio, where the group would have to record enough material for a first album. The preparations were extensive, but when the finished product was presented to the world in 1978, no one could get enough of this latest teen sensation.

That summer, Menudo had firmly incorporated themselves as the first Latin pop group to move into America's musical mainstream. With their first stop in New York City, Menudo made quite a splash with U.S. audiences, appearing in such popular programs and events as *Good Morning America*, *Solid Gold*, *20/20*, *Silver Spoons*, *The Love Boat*, Macy's parade, and the Grammys.

In 1983, the group was at the pinnacle of their success. Similar to the Beatles, Menudo had launched their own brand of mania. Producing one record-breaking album after another in English, Spanish, Portuguese, and Tagalo, the band of teenagers were even given star billing in a feature film that set a box office record at New York's famed Latin Theatre.

After five years of nonstop touring and recording, the Menudo phenomenon had not lost any of its thunder. Their concerts were so jam-packed that Menudo earned the Guinness World of Records' top three spots for largest audiences in 1983. Whether they were being swarmed by 105,000 fans in Mexico City's Azteca Stadium or making the rounds through some of the U.S.'s most prestigious venues, Menudo proved that they had the stuff that legends were made of.

Nineteen years and thirty-three prepubescent Latino members later, the group has recorded thirty-one albums with total sales of over $20 million. The Menudo tradition, however, would not be thwarted. Although the group would eventually lose favor with American audiences in the 1990s, it found a new calling under the name of MDO. Today, the MDO quintet continues to dominate the airwaves of Central and South America, infusing sold-out auditoriums with a dynamic blend of Latin pop and rhythm.

When Ricky joined the group in the fall of 1983, Menudo was commercially positioned for greatness in the U.S. and around the world. That fact could explain why the search for Ricky Melendez's replacement took so long. With their reign over the pop charts progressing so seamlessly, Diaz couldn't risk choosing someone incapable of toeing the Menudo line and further the Menudo agenda. The lucky winner had to be a consummate professional and would have to have a way with the female fans. Ricky's non-threatening, boy-next-door demeanor would work wonders on the younger spectators. For many girls, he was just what the pediatrician ordered.

After leaving home for Orlando (the location of Menudo's training facility) Ricky was anxious to get on stage and work his magic. While his heart was definitely in the right place, he still had so much left to learn. Having passed the audition, he assumed that the biggest challenge was now behind him, and was not prepared for all that the next year would bring. Getting ushered into the Menudo compound, he was quickly informed that he could not perform with the group until he completed the requisite training sessions. Though Ricky was surprised at the revelation, he was a good sport, willing to do anything for his chance to be part of the Menudo phenomenon.

Instead of the summer camp-like experience he'd envisioned, being a part of Menudo required immense discipline and hard work. During 1984, Ricky paralleled his life in Menudo to that of a soldier in boot camp. The boys had a strict schedule and code of conduct. They were required to be prompt, professional, and courteous at all times.

A day in the life of the young trainee would start early in the morning with breakfast, then it was off to dance class, followed by vocal coaching, and even media training. As a member of Menudo, Ricky would not only have to know his way around a concert hall, but also a press conference. Being that he was still a minor, Ricky was also forced to complete his academic courses. When it came to molding his boys into stars, Diaz spared no expense. Private tutors, top-notch choreographers, and leading voice trainers guided Ricky's every step. "I had to learn for a whole year before I first got on a stage," he revealed to *Salut*. "It was very hard: I had singing and dancing lessons every single day and I had a private teacher for the other subjects that kids are supposed to learn in school."

Of course, all work and no play could make for grumpy Menudos. To keep the group from turning on their exacting management, the boys were given free time to hang out, watch television, and frequent the local hot spots. While he may have felt like a foot soldier with the Menudo army, Ricky was the furthest thing from a prisoner of the pop wars. "Yes, Menudo was like going to a military academy," he confessed to *Estylo*. "The managers and the people who were responsible for us, they were strong on our growth. They were dealing with kids and there was a lot of work to do. But they knew how to divide friendship, fun, and work. For me, that's discipline. When you're working you're working and you have to be focused. There is a time to party and play and a time to work. I am very grateful because they taught me how important it is to be focused and to this day I follow that.''

No matter how tired he was or how much he complained, Ricky knew that the instruction was for his own good. Few boys his age could boast such an extensive knowledge of the music industry. Always a quick study, he passed his training with flying colors. He was now ready to move on to the next level—performing before à live audience.

While Ricky was comfortable showcasing his talents in front of crowds, he couldn't have predicted the rush that prancing in front of thousands of Menudo fans would produce. When he took to the stage for the first time, the cheering and clapping, as well as the flowers and gifts streaming through the air, caused him to go faint from fear. The adrenaline rush of being loved by so many people was just too much for his sensitive soul to bear. At once the happiest and the most frightening moment of Ricky's life, his first performance left an indelible impression that he would not soon forget.

Initially, he was terrified by the riotous commotion brought about by Menudo's song and dance act. Nonetheless, he couldn't wait to come back for more. He described that first encounter with the public to *Salut*: ''It was on July 10, 1984, in Puerto Rico, and I was very nervous. I only had two songs to sing with my then-group, Menudo. I was a nervous wreck, but when I got off stage, I wanted to go back so bad! Thankfully, my second concert in New York was two hours long!''

Once the hoopla had died down and the boys of Menudo retired backstage, Ricky was congratulated for a job well done. His brief but memorable contribution to the concert was duly noted by each group member, including the manager. Ricky had passed the trial-by-fire with flying colors, and was now a full-fledged member of the Menudo clan.

Reeling for hours after the performance, Ricky couldn't fall asleep no matter how hard he tried. He kept replaying the applause of the audience in his mind, unable to believe that some of it was for him. His state of mind bordered on the ecstatic. That show had opened up a can of worms that would forever remain ajar. To this day, he derives incredible joy from each and every heart-stopping performance. And like his twelve-year-old counterpart, Ricky still has trouble falling asleep after a long night of dance and music.

Having effortlessly sailed through his first show, Ricky was swept up in the whirl of a Menudo world tour. Life on the road with the group was everything he had expected and more. Flying from one country to another, posing for myriad photographers, and answering hundreds of questions for curious reporters, Ricky was moving at a breakneck pace and loving every hectic minute of it. The constant change and variety was extremely appealing to the young singer. He enjoyed going around each hemisphere in a matter of days, hanging out with his pals in the group, and meeting his fans. While some performers quickly tire of the barrage of promotional appearances, Ricky thrived in this setting. "I've learned a lot of things and seen lots of fabulous places," he told *Salut*. "While my friends were back home and learning the geography of Japan at school, I was on stage in Tokyo! I had to grow up fast, but I was still in a sane environment and I wish everyone could have lived the same things I lived through Menudo."

Ricky's dream of seeing the world was finally realized. Fascinated with different cultures and religions, the constant travel afforded him the kind of education he would never have gotten in a regular school. Instead of shunning his fans as most busy pop stars are apt to do, Ricky jumped at the opportunity to learn from them. His voracious appetite for learning and education didn't subside just because he had struck it big as a performer.

As a member of Menudo, it was all too easy to get swept away by the hype and excitement. Keeping a solid, grounded outlook on life was virtually impossible. With so many fans willing to lay down their lives for each and every member of the Menudo posse, some of Ricky's band mates developed oversized egos. Ricky, however, made an effort to focus on the important things in life. As any VH-1 *Behind the Music* special will show, the task proved well-nigh impossible. Were it not for the aid of his family, his lavish pop band experience might have cost him his future. "We were treated very well and we were with great people as well," he reminisced about his Menudo years with *Salut*. "We had a maid, a lady who was like our nanny, and a choreographer, José Luis (we've known each other for thirteen years now and he has became my assistant). I was a kid and, all of a sudden, I found myself in a world where we rode in limos, stayed in the best hotels and got to perform in front of thousands of screaming girls. But I think I got out of it with my head still on my shoulders."

What made Ricky's romp through the world with Menudo even better was his friendship with the other group members. Extremely social from an early age, he wasted no time before bonding with his new comrades. Because he was much younger than the rest of the guys, he was treated like a little brother. Whenever he would get depressed, scared, or homesick, Ricky could count on his new friends to extend a helping hand. Since they were older, more experienced, and, in some cases, wiser, their advice and attention helped him weather the bad times. The friendships he developed were so strong that Ricky still finds himself thinking about the glory days. "I miss my sweet sixteen," he lamented to *Salut*. "We had so much fun at the time: we were a bunch of friends, together 24/7 and we had nothing to worry about. Today, my friends are what I miss most to be completely happy. So I need to count on my old memories to fulfill that emptiness."

The closeness between the group never subsided, even when some of the group members would get more attention in the public eye. When Ricky first hit the scene, people didn't know what to make of him. Visibly small and extremely adorable, he was considered to be the resident cutie pie, a label that didn't sit too well with him. "And you had favorites within the group," he confirmed to the *Los Angeles Times*. "Some were favored by the fans, and some were favored by the managers. There were many things going on. I was a very small kid, twelve years old but I looked like I was eight. So with me, the fans would say, 'Who's that little one, the cute one?' "

As he developed into the mature and well-built man he is today, Ricky began melting more hearts than any of the other members. After just two short years with the group, he had become the most popular Menudoan around. And considering the group's overall success, that was no small accomplishment. In fact, it was almost more than Ricky could bear. At one point, nearly 2,000 Menudo fans began tearing at the boys' clothes during an autograph session in San Antonio, Texas. The incident was so startling, auxiliary police officers had to be called in to contain the damage. This frenzied mauling of Menudo was branded by both CNN and *Entertainment Tonight* as a sign of Spanish Beatlemania. Instantly recognizable to throngs of worshippers, Ricky couldn't go anywhere for fear of being assailed by his fans. In the end, however, he didn't begrudge the loss of his privacy. Instead, he played up his popularity, winking at the girls onstage and off.

Speaking of girls, at one point or another many people have wondered about Menudo's romantic exploits. Were they truly the Latin Romeos they claimed to be? Was it true that they had their pick of girls at any concert? The answer to these questions is a resounding "Yes." The Menudo boys lived up to and even exceeded their bad-boy reputations. After every concert, Menudo groupies would line up backstage hoping to get a date with one of the members. Despite the presence of a nanny on tour, the guys found ample opportunity to enjoy the wine, women, and song lifestyle.

While Ricky may have wanted to meet girls when he first joined Menudo, even he was shocked to find out what really went on in the green rooms. It was truly a parent's worst nightmare. Seeing that he was only twelve years old, Ricky postponed his sexual awakening until he was more mature. "When I was younger, during my Menudo years, I met millions of girls," he revealed to *Star Club*. "The other band members brought some fans back to our hotel room and made love to them. And sometimes right before my eyes! I never needed sex ed class. I stayed in my little corner, I had no choice: I felt I was too young to have sex. But the circumstances didn't quite delight me."

As Ricky matured into full-blown adolescence, the sexual escapades lost some of their initial shock value. In fact, he admitted to having a liaison or two of his own during his tenure with Menudo. Yet, while he acknowledges having had relations with his fair share of female fans, he is not proud of his behavior. Today Ricky is a new man, placing a greater emphasis on the quality rather than quantity of his relationships. "It was crazy! I didn't have to do much for girls to go after me," he told *Salut*. "And I took advantage of it, but I changed when I turned eighteen. Now, I want stability in a relationship, I don't want one-night stands. But I have absolutely no regrets about the good times I've had thanks to Menudo!"

To the casual observer, touring with Menudo seemed like nothing but good times and hearty laughs. Of course, even the glamorous life was not without its own share of problems. At first sight, Ricky fell head over heels in love with the Menudo lifestyle. But as he grew older and wiser, he developed a more mature outlook on his surroundings. One of Ricky's concerns was his lack of creative control. It seems that Diaz had his own vision of what the group should look, act, and sound like. Through the years, Ricky began feeling stifled by the image he was being forced to portray. Describing the group as a "concept" he went on to tell *People* magazine, "Our creativity was stifled. We were told [the songs we wrote] were no good. We began to question the need for rehearsing the same routines over and over."

Short of staging an all-out insurrection, there was really nothing Ricky or the boys could do. They had signed away their independence, and were contractually bound to cooperate with the management and follow their rules. No contract, however, could stop hot-tempered Ricky from trying to get his way. The battle of wills would continue for many years, until the day Ricky turned seventeen and had to bid the group adieu.

To be fair, if not for the Menudo experience, Ricky might not be the incredibly successful man that he is today. While he was forced to give up some artistic control in the process and forsake typical childhood activities like going to dances and hanging out at the mall, the positive aspects of being a part of the Menudo phenomenon outweighed the negative. "My school has been the hotel room and the lobby has been my playground," he said. "But I have no regrets, it has been a fascinating journey. I experienced firsthand what I would need to know when I went solo. It taught me to be disciplined, something that I still practice today."

Ricky couldn't have asked for a better way of life. From an early age, his every wish was someone else's command. Deprivation was a concept completely foreign to him. But it wasn't only Menudo that fostered his self-confidence and high-maintenance personality. His parents had been spoiling him long before his days as a teen idol. Part of what made him so lovable to the fans was the faith that his parents had instilled in him. And since family had played such a vital role in his life, its absence left him feeling disoriented and downcast. As visits home became fewer and increasingly far between, his parents ached for the loss of their son. Even though they had other children to keep them jumping through hoops, Ricky had a knack for bringing joy and laughter everywhere he went. When he went away to become one of the reigning princes of the international music scene, it was all they could do to keep from calling him every day.

At first, the tragedy of losing their son drew the divorced parents closer together. Enrique and Nereida turned to each other for much-needed consolation during the initial phase of Ricky's musical career. But as his absence became more pronounced, the two began fighting over visitation rights. Every hour seemed precious to the desolate parents, and there were no lengths to which they wouldn't go to monopolize Ricky's time at home.

The knowledge that he was the source of family discord sat none too well with the prodigal son. Although he was having the time of his life, he spent many sleepless nights worrying about his parents' welfare. Despite his best efforts, Ricky was incapable of alleviating the discord. If he tried to go home more often, he would have to face the daunting task of getting past Menudo's management. If he quit the group, he would feel like he had squandered the most important career break of his life. It was truly a no-win situation. "When my dreams started coming true," he explained to *People*, "my parents started fighting. I had everything I ever wanted, but my family was falling apart. Before that, I was the glue that kept them friendly toward each other."

After deliberating endlessly with little success, his father laid down a rather harsh ultimatum that neither Ricky nor Nereida were prepared to handle. Enrique was so tired of the constant bickering, he decided that their son would have to choose one parent as his sole guardian. He "wanted me to choose between him and my mother," Ricky later fumed. "How do you ask a child that?"

At first, Ricky refused to take his father seriously. He hoped that time would bring about a more rational and equitable solution to their conflict. But when no such resolution seemed forthcoming, the young performer was forced to reevaluate the custody arrangement. Ricky tried to reason with his father at every turn, even going so far as to promise to increase his visits home. No arguments, however, could sway Enrique. The equally hardheaded Ricky refused to compromise. If his father was so callous about his devotion, then Ricky felt that he wasn't deserving of it in the first place.

The ensuing rift between father and son was irreparable. Ricky was furious with the blatant contempt his father had shown him. After all, he had done nothing wrong, and believed that he was being unjustly punished. In 1985, he was so angry with his father, he even went so far as to legally change his name from Enrique. His mother was disappointed with the outcome of the family feud, but supported Ricky's decision. It would be nine years before Ricky would speak to his father again.

Coping with the recent estrangement from his father became even more difficult as Ricky tried to hide his pain from the group and himself. His efforts to convince himself that the separation was for the best were futile. Even as he was bringing joy to people all around the world, Ricky was devastated by the loss. He had grown up thinking that his family would always stand by him no matter what happened, and he was not equipped to deal with the far grimmer reality.

In order to cope with the loss of his father, Ricky threw himself into his work. He committed himself to the group, finding solace in the all-consuming performance schedule. Had it not been for the emotional outlet Menudo provided, Ricky might well have fallen victim to the ravages of the family storm. Luckily, he had the unconditional devotion of his group members and fans to elevate his sunken spirits.

The next three years saw Ricky traveling the world and enjoying everything the music industry had to offer. He was so wrapped up in being a part of Menudo that he lost sight of the fact that it would one day all come to a screeching halt. The Menudo rules were written in stone. As soon as a member turned seventeen, he had to leave the group, no questions asked. This commandment could not be broken, even by Ricky, who had by then, established himself as one of the most popular members of the group. Although the world would hate to see him go, his departure was as inevitable as the sunset.

Reflecting upon the happy times he shared with the group, Ricky started to worry about the prospect of bidding it all a fond farewell. The Menudo phase had been such a long and wonderful ride that he'd become completely wrapped up in the experience. Ricky honestly never gave the rest of his life much thought. As the last of his Menudo days neared, the uncertainty of the future became a source of much consternation.

During his final concert with the group, Ricky was an emotional wreck. Not until the bitter end did he realize exactly how attached he had become to the group and the manager. As he went through the all-too familiar motions of the concert, Ricky was smiling through his tears. Only then did he truly understand what Menudo had meant to him. This was one poignant moment that would haunt him for the rest of his life. "I was in Menudo between the ages of twelve and seventeen. It was a phenomenal experience," he reminisced with *Smash Hits*. "Unfortunately, the Menudo rule was that you had to leave the band once you reached seventeen. The last concert was in Puerto Rico, my home town. I am a man who cries, and I cried a lot.''

The pain of losing his father and his best friends in such a short span of time was all too much. Stumbling backstage, Ricky broke down and cried like a child. While his childhood friends from San Juan had suffered their school years by counting the days, his five-year musical education seemed to have flown by in the blink of an eye. The idea that some new member would be replacing him was understandably painful. Menudo had become synonymous with the best part of his youth, and leaving the group meant that he had finally grown into a man. This sudden insight put Ricky on edge. While the group had afforded him many great opportunities and he would miss it dearly, it was the fear of the unknown that really gave him something to cry about.

After he had shed his last tear, packed his last bag, and uttered his last goodbye, Ricky was left alone with his thoughts. Finally, he could really sit down and reflect on the past five years. Although he had changed so much, the fast pace of his former lifestyle had prevented him from coming to terms with the responsibilities of his burgeoning manhood. For the first time, Ricky thought long and hard about his life. Besides discovering that leaving Menudo was actually a blessing in disguise, he also learned that he was confident about the next phase of his life. "I was part of the group for five years and then I left," he told *Hitkrant*. "As great as it was, I felt that it was time to move on. I was exhausted! But the Menudo-period was great. If a member of a boy group reads this, let me give you a tip: use every second that you are part of the group. You learn from everything and when it's over you can use that knowledge and go and do whatever you want.

You have to make people see you as more than just part of that group. I'd hate to still be called Ricky 'ex-Menudo' Martin. But if you go and do new things yourself, that will pass. You just have to prove that you can do more than perform in that group.''

Since he had squeezed an awful lot of living into a short period of time, Ricky had gained the tools to handle anything that life threw his way. The fact that he didn't know what he wanted to do next failed to upset him. Through his meanderings with Menudo he had made a lot of money. Now he could sit back and figure out what he was really meant to do. And while he wouldn't figure out his life's purpose overnight, he was as confident as ever that he would succeed in whatever field he chose. ''Menudo has been the best school for me. When I left the band, I was able to fight everything,'' he confided in *Star Club*. ''If I'd wanted to be a doctor, I would have been an excellent doctor. Or an excellent engineer . . . I don't see myself as more or less cultivated than the majority.''

By the time he had sorted through all of his feelings about Menudo, Ricky was tired of dwelling on the past and ready to dive headlong into the future. Having placed Menudo in its proper perspective, he decided that while it was a great learning experience, he wouldn't consider a reunion any time soon. The recent reunification of his fellow Menudo members showed Ricky that he was very much over that phase of his life. And even though he supports the group, he is glad he left when he did. ''It's something I would never do,'' Ricky conveyed to the *Los Angeles Times*. ''But let's be clear about it. I am Latin American and I know how important that group was for a whole generation of people. If everybody is having a good time, if the guys on stage are enjoying it, and the people who go see them have fun remembering the old times, I have no problem whatsoever with it.''

The most difficult, memorable, and emotionally charged years of his life were spent alongside the boys of Menudo. Along the way, Ricky had made some mistakes and come to grips with his own humanity. The lessons he learned and the facts of life he uncovered through trial and error only served to humble him further. Although he'd been worshipped by millions of fans from every continent, he quickly abandoned the image that propelled him to stardom.

Instead of coming out of the experience feeling like the world owed him a favor, Ricky did something completely unexpected. He retired into a realm he had neglected for too long; a realm of imagination and creativity. Having spent nearly one third of his seventeen years on the road, in the recording studio or surrounded by reporters, he was relieved to find that he had emerged unscathed and optimistic. "I gave Menudo all I had, and when I felt it was the moment to part with them, I left completely convinced that I was ready for another stage of both my career and my life.''

CHAPTER 3

On His Own

The childlike Ricky of the past had vanished. In his place, however, appeared a man with immense character, conviction, and purpose. Instead of charging full-force into another musical group or trying to get a leg up in the show business community, Ricky returned to Puerto Rico in order to complete his high school education. While his move was a blessing for his mother and grandmother, his friends likened it to career suicide. Menudo had opened up a world of possibilities to Ricky. Now that he was a free agent, he could start his own group or even tour the world as a solo artist. But no amount of persuasion could change Ricky's mind. He was fed up with both the agony and the ecstasy of touring the world, and wished for nothing more than to temper his otherwise chaotic existence with an element of normality.

The opposition Ricky encountered from his musical colleagues wasn't completely out of left field. After all, Menudo could have been his ticket to bigger and better things. Without the proper guidance, many feared that Ricky would become a has-been and live out the rest of his days in total obscurity. Paying little attention to all the naysayers, Ricky had faith in his ability to orchestrate a comeback, when and if he ever chose to. His decision to return to his homeland was one of the soundest he had ever made.

Upon arriving at the airport, Ricky was welcomed back into the family with open arms. A celebratory mood pervaded the terminal. It was as if Ricky had come home from serving an extended tour of duty in the military. There was, however, one blemish on the face of the otherwise joyful day. His father failed to put in an appearance. Thankfully, the excitement of coming home overshadowed the potential disappointment. Ricky had been deeply missed, and rejoiced in the love of his nearest and dearest.

Nothing could rival the emotion he experienced upon entering his house and realizing that he would soon know the joyous comfort of waking up in the same bed every day. During the past five years, Ricky had forgotten the benefits of leading a stable, immobile lifestyle. It seemed that the security he felt in his birth home was all he would ever need, until, that is, he grew restless and renewed his search for meaning.

With graduation came an important decision. Ricky struggled with the responsibility of generating a life-plan. The options were limitless, and that was exactly what worried him most. "When I left the group Menudo, I was totally disoriented," said Ricky. "I didn't know what would happen, nor what I wanted out of my life. I thought of coming back to school to study dramatic arts or something like communication."

Even as his family urged him to pursue a higher education, Ricky held to his belief that doing nothing was exactly what the doctor ordered. A deeply thoughtful and analytic young man, he craved the solitude forsaken during the Menudo era. Once left to his own devices, he was convinced that he'd uncover the direction his life was meant to take. For Ricky, the search for his true calling would have to take precedence over everything else, including his mother's wishes. "I wanted to get to know myself," he explained to the *Los Angeles Times*, "because the first five years of my career had been a nonstop barrage of euphoria and adrenaline and a lot of mixed feelings."

Although Puerto Rico would always be his real home, Ricky felt that he needed to escape the trappings of his childhood in order to discover the man he was meant to be. To that end, he decided to leave for New York City. During his career with Menudo, Ricky visited Manhattan on several occasions, falling in love with what little of it he saw. Its pulsating rhythm and the diversity of its populace drew Ricky like a moth to a flame. Anything was possible in New York, even reinventing himself. So after graduating from high school, Ricky packed his bags, telling his mother it would only be for a short while.

Nerieda, however, wasn't sold on the idea. She tried to impress upon Ricky the importance of staying in Puerto Rico after his five-year absence. But when he told her he would be returning soon, she agreed to let him go. The pain of losing her boy the second time around was tremendous. No sooner had he come back into her life, than he was gone again just as quickly. Since he was determined to make it on his own, his mother threw up her hands and gave him her blessing.

New York City was everything Ricky remembered it to be. Although he had traveled extensively with Menudo, this was the first trip he had taken by himself. At last, he was the one calling all the shots. Of course, he had no idea where to go, where to stay, or whom to associate with. He didn't know a solitary soul in Manhattan. But that was exactly what made the trip so exhilarating. If he made a mistake, it would be his own fault. If he accomplished something great, he would only have himself to thank. His newfound independence was the greatest gift he had ever received, and he wasn't about to give it up without a fight.

The excitement he felt upon deplaning in New York motivated him to call his mother and tell her that he would be staying indefinitely. Her shock was considerable. She begged him to reconsider, even suggesting Miami, which was a much closer alternative. "I was seventeen years old and I'd just moved to New York, alone," he told *Cleo*. "I told my mother I was going to New York for a vacation. Then, when I landed at the airport, I called her and told her I was staying. She went crazy."

Nerieda couldn't have known that no amount of exhortation would change her son's mind. New York had an allure all its own, and Ricky was hooked. What had begun as a holiday, a mere exploratory voyage, had turned into the ultimate challenge—self-reliance. He described his first activities to *Cleo*, "I started looking for an apartment, furniture, and things, but it was when I opened an account and signed the first check for the rent that I thought, 'Okay, this is it, I'm on my own now.' It felt amazing."

The rush of liberation was too intense a feeling to ignore. Ricky reveled in the most mundane activities like doing his own laundry, cooking for himself, and cleaning his new apartment. Settling into his first home, he believed that he had finally become a man. He had paid his own way, and wouldn't dream of asking for assistance. This rugged self-sufficiency was a source of considerable pride. "I did a lot of growing up there," Ricky asserted to *People*. "In Menudo they told you what silverware to use. Suddenly I was paying my own bills.''

While some newcomers to Manhattan feel overwhelmed by its size and pace, Ricky savored the city's atmosphere. He loved New York so much that he decided to brave all the thrills and chills it had to offer. The only way to do that, however, was to give himself up to the town's natural flow. Work was simply out of the question. Whether he was strolling through the parks, eating at one of the famous delis, or visiting the local galleries, Ricky was captivated with every sight, sound, and sensation. ''Well, I went to New York and there I did absolutely nothing,'' he described the experience to *Hitkrant*. ''That was great! I just sat myself down on a bench and watched the people . . . I really needed to be alone.''

By putting the brakes on his ambitions and committing himself to a life of leisure, Ricky tapped into a part of himself he thought he had lost forever. As a member of Menudo, every minute of every hour was accounted for. The freedom most people take for granted, to explore their thoughts or just be themselves, had been significantly curtailed. In New York, however, he could be whoever he wanted, come and go as he pleased, as well as meet people from a variety of backgrounds. Although Ricky kept to himself for the most part, he did make some new friends who were instrumental in showing him around the town.

Whereas loneliness had proved to be an elusive sensation for the always resourceful young man, the need to be active and make something out of his life slowly crept up on him. After six months of walking the streets and painting a new mental picture of the world, Ricky had to admit that the routine was becoming a bit tedious. He was finally rejuvenated and ready to exercise

his talents and faculties. The only question remaining
was *how?* "I was actually still deciding whether I
would continue in show business, because I had found
a lot of success already," Ricky explained to *Hitkrant*.

Actually, it was Ricky's mother that kept pushing
him to reenter the world of show business. A woman
of great common sense, Nereida could not fathom why
a gifted performer like Ricky would waste his time
playing the vagabond. During their long weekly conversations, Nereida prodded her son to get off his laurels and strive to achieve something of substance.
"There was only one person who kept telling me, 'You
gotta go back on stage,'" he told the *Los Angeles
Times*. "It was my mother, always there, bugging me
the way only she can. And I would tell her, 'Mom, I'm
never going back on stage.' It took me only a year to
go back."

Without his mother's not-so-gentle prodding, Ricky
might very well have given up on music and acting all
together. But as a loyal and loving son, he took his
mother's advice to heart. It was important, however,
that Ricky not rush his return to the stage. He wanted
to get his feet wet as a model first, and set off to conquer the rarefied world of fashion.

Although Ricky's diminutive frame had raised some
eyebrows at the Menudo audition, his subsequent years
with the group had seen him grow into the quintessence
of tall, dark, and handsome. His strong, lean jaw and
hard body were his entrée into the elite circles. While
New York agencies can be very exclusive and selec-
tive, Ricky was instantly invited to join. It was not
much later that he had an impressive portfolio to show
off to his new friends.

Almost immediately, his days became taken up by
smiling or smoldering for the camera. Decorating a

room, or a billboard for that matter, was far from the be-all-end-all of Ricky's existence. He decided to advance his education as a performer with acting and dancing classes. By applying himself to his studies, he impressed his instructors with his dedication and natural abilities. It wasn't so much the classes themselves that interested Ricky, but the feeling of performing onstage in front of the class. After experiencing so much joy from being in the spotlight almost every night with Menudo, he had grown accustomed to the highs and lows of a performer's life. When he acknowledged how much he looked forward to acting in front of his classmates every night, Ricky couldn't deny the thrill of performance any longer. "I took acting lessons and that's when I understood I wanted to stay in the business," he relayed to *Salut*.

Coming to New York to find himself, Ricky discovered that he had known who he was all along. What he really needed and received was time away from the rigors of show business. Time to simply unwind, relax, and take a long, deep breath. Having done precisely that, Ricky was now excited to find out what was waiting for him around the corner. As luck would have it, he wouldn't have to wait long. Just as he had grown bored with being a fashion plate and decided to return to acting, a producer from Mexico called him in for an audition. Coincidentally, his old friends from Menudo had just invited him to join them on their vacation in Mexico City. Seeing as he missed his friends and was on the look out for acting roles, Ricky had no trouble making the decision.

Having sowed his proverbial oats in Manhattan, Ricky had had his fill of the United States. He longed to travel closer to home, and Mexico City would afford him the luxury of developing his career and maintaining close contact with his family. The call from the producer had been a relief. He had considered acting full-time in New York, but his heart wasn't in it. Taking the call from the Mexican producer as a sign, he was certain that the right way to go was south.

When he informed his mother of his new plans, she was elated by the prospect. Missing Ricky had become a habit, but not one she wouldn't gladly break. She advised her son to make the transition, even helping him make all the travel arrangements. So after locking up his apartment and saying goodbye to a handful of friends, Ricky was off to embark on yet another wonderful adventure.

Mexico City was a far cry from what he had envisioned. Instead of the old-fashioned pueblo environs he had expected, he was thrilled to find himself smack dab in the middle of a bustling and totally cosmopolitan metropolis. Unfortunately, Ricky would not have the chance to take in the sights as he had during his trip to New York. He barely had enough time to adapt to his new surroundings, because as soon as his feet touched the soil, he was off to audition for the long-running musical, *Mamá Ama el Rock* (*Mom Loves Rock*) starring Angélica Vale and Angélica María.

Clinching the coveted role was a much simpler proposition than he had imagined. Unbeknownst to Ricky, he was virtually guaranteed the part. After the producer watched Ricky's concerts with Menudo and his early commercial work, he was blown away by the performer's range and abilities. Ricky, meanwhile, had no idea of the impression he'd made. Hoping that he hadn't come all this way for nothing, he went all out to secure the role. He was, of course, offered the job. He counted on the play's success to launch his acting career and signed on the dotted line without much hesitation.

His next order of business was to find a place to stay. Unlike his visit to New York, Ricky would not be on his own this time. With many friends living in the area, all the arrangements fell into place. Through a mutual acquaintance, he met and moved in with a group of people who would become some of his closest friends. "I had a lot of friends and I was kind of adopted by this incredible family," he explained during an America Online chat. "They made it so much easier, but I got used to it easily, because I was working a lot. It was so different just being in another country where Spanish is spoken, but it's almost another language. I would go back there anytime."

In May of 1990, Ricky was once again living the good life. After being secluded in New York City for so long, he became quite social and embraced his regained popularity. Mexico City offered him everything he was looking for. With a population of millions, the city provided a neverending supply of entertainment possibilities. Known as the center of Mexican life, its famous monuments, palaces, museums, nightclubs, and shops draw a steady supply of tourists each year.

A city boy through and through, Ricky's only complaint with his new conditions was not having enough time for himself. Once again, the demands of singing, acting, and dancing in one of the city's most popular musicals weighed heavily on his shoulders. That's not to say that he didn't enjoy his comeback to the stage. *Mamá Ama el Rock* introduced Ricky to the musical theater, an art form he's loved ever since. The complexity of combining his singing and acting skills proved much to his liking, and he worked diligently at honing his craft and perfecting his delivery onstage.

While New York had provided the solitude he needed, Ricky would always be a showman by nature. His longing for making crowds jump to their feet never subsided. Rejuvenated by his onstage success, Ricky thought that he found his true calling at last. But as all good things must come to an end, his days in the theater were numbered.

Fortunately, Ricky would never have to resort to singing for his supper on street corners and bus terminals. He had gained significant exposure through his mesmerizing performances with *Mamá Ama el Rock*, and no sooner had the show run its course than casting directors were already queuing up at his door. Since the offers were pouring in, Ricky decided to weigh his options carefully. He couldn't afford to be careless at this tender juncture of his career. Making a name for himself would require a consistent selection of worthwhile projects that would highlight and not detract from his skills as an actor and singer.

The choice hadn't been an easy one to make, but Ricky decided to sign an eight-month contract to play a leading role in the popular Spanish soap opera or telenovela *Alcanzar Una Estrella II* (*To Reach a Star*). While the show's perpetually high ratings played a part in his decision, it was really the role of Pablo that convinced him to make the commitment. A musician and singer with the band Muñecos de Papel, Pablo reminded Ricky of himself. He, too, was a sensitive and romantic singer trying to make a name for himself.

When the fictional band launched a very real tour through Mexico, Ricky had the chance to merge his greatest passions into one exciting experience. "I did a musical, so I didn't have to turn my back on music," he confirmed to *Hitkrant*. "While I was working in the theater, someone called me and asked me to do some

TV work. It was a soap. I played a musician, so I could keep on singing. I also did the title song of that series.''

The drama's success led Ricky to bigger things. The group Muñecos de Papel developed quite a following in Mexico, leading the show's producers to create an album in which each actor contributed a song. Ricky's song, ''Juego de Ajedrez,'' was a major hit with fans from the beginning. The passion and feeling he invested into each note captivated audiences young and old alike.

A commercial triumph, the album showed that the thirst for all things *Alcanzar Una Estrella II* was truly unquenchable. To appease the public, the producers decided to take the show onto the big screen with the film spin-off *Mas Que Alcanzar Una Estrella*. More accolades were soon to follow. Ricky's performance in the feature was unanimously praised by critics. He was branded one of the film's breakout stars, and earned the prestigious *Premio Heraldo* (Mexico's version of the Academy Award).

The year of 1991 had been extremely good to Ricky. When he landed in Mexico City, he didn't know what to expect from his stay. He didn't even know how long he would call the city home. All he knew for certain was that he was being given a rare shot to shine as an actor. In one year's time, he had gone from modeling to musical theater to feature films, and showed the people of Mexico the full extent of his talent in the process. More important, however, Ricky realized that he could live up to the expectations he had set for himself. For a while there, he'd felt like a quitter. Lacking the motivation to so much as look for a job, he'd harbored many a doubt about his future.

While paying his dues as the new kid on the Mexican block, Ricky was once again inspired to become

an artist. Menudo's many demands and restrictions had
robbed him of his pure love for performance and the
arts. Through his work on television and the theater,
however, Ricky reclaimed his rightful passion for song
and dance. He rediscovered what it was that had drawn
him to a musician's life in the first place. "There,
everything that I did in acting had to do with music,"
he explained. "I participated in a soap opera, *Alcanzar
Una Estrella II*, where I also sang the theme song; and
I acted in a show called *Mom Loves Rock* and that
fascinated me."

Despite his early days in Menudo, going from a successful gig as an actor to a career in music required great
faith and courage. Thanks to the critical and commercial
success of his recent projects, Ricky had the strength to
work harder and dream bigger. After winning the Heraldo, he was propelled into a new realm of activity.
Countless fans and reporters wanted to know what the
sexy young performer would do next. After hearing his
moving contribution to the album *Muñecos de Papel*,
many hoped that he would record a solo album. And
that's precisely what Ricky went on to do.

Ricky's rise to fame as a solo artist began humbly and
without much fanfare. As a permanent fixture in the
public eye, he discussed his love for music and touring
on infinite occasions. After hearing him express his desire to go solo, an executive from Sony Music México
contacted the young man and offered him a record contract. Not for one minute did Ricky so much as consider
turning down the offer. Ever since performing with the
group Muñecos de Papel had revived his love of touring and song, Ricky had wanted little else. "Later I
devoted myself completely to music. Being on stage
with the group Muñecos de Papel, which drew crowds

of up to 65,000 people for a single concert, I realized that my calling was music, what a beautiful thing it was to sing. That's where it all began.''

The opportunity to distance himself even further from Menudo was very tempting. Since many of his interviews still dwelled on his ''checkered'' past, a solo album seemed like just the thing to cut the umbilical cord between himself and the group once and for all. While the cute antics of Menudo's little Ricky had been fine for a teenager, he needed to create something that better reflected the man he had become. ''When I came back to the spotlight I had a completely different image,'' he relayed to *Latin Music Online*. ''In Latin America, they don't remember me as being with Menudo. I was a little kid in Menudo, I had long hair, and it was a different point of view.''

Becoming a solo artist also meant that Ricky would have more control over his music. Since he had been excluded from the creative process during his years as a teen heartthrob, Ricky was that much more anxious to steer the production of his album. Whether it was writing a song or mixing a track, he was involved every step of the way. Watching him work in the studio, no one could have guessed that he was a novice. Although he had not been allowed to provide feedback before, he'd had plenty of chances to observe every aspect of Menudo's recording sessions. By watching and listening carefully to the goings on in the control rooms, Ricky had picked up valuable knowledge. Once it was time to record his own music, he astounded the producers. This was one guy who knew his way around a studio and a sound board. ''It felt great to have complete control of the process,'' explained Ricky. ''I was also lucky to be surrounded by people who wanted to work as hard as I did.''

Despite his sweet façade, Ricky was no pushover. The pressure to ante up a stellar debut forced him to take charge, and even crack the whip once in a while. The words "second chance" had no place in his vocabulary. He would either do it right the first time, or not at all. Even though his temperament would get the better of him every now and then, Ricky never let good enough alone. If Menudo had taught him anything, it was that hard work and discipline were necessary to achieve excellence. "In the studio, I'm very demanding toward myself, so I am toward others as well," he asserted to *Star Club*. "I mean that if a sound take is not done well enough, for example, I do it all over again or I have it redone if I'm the one who pays for it. What I don't accept is amateurism, and when it's not right, I don't pretend it is."

While working on his debut album, Ricky also had the chance to get reacquainted with creative writing. As a young boy, his grandmother taught him to compose lyrics and write poetry. He had always been a gifted writer, but as the years passed, Ricky had less and less time to devote to this interest. When the occasion to contribute original songs arose, Ricky made his move. Secluding himself in his room for hours on end, he labored over every verse until he was satisfied with the results. He even shared his lyrics with his grandmother, listening to and incorporating the constructive criticism she generously provided. "Sometimes I don't know how, but when I sit down to write lyrics, what I want to talk about in a song," Ricky told *Latin Music Online*, "it is beautiful to write, to sing your own music, you know what you're talking about, you know what you're saying."

As luck would have it, love for a woman was the emotion Ricky felt most in touch with at the time.

Judging by the ballad-rich content of his album, the woman in question was an important fixture in his life. Rebeca de Alba, a popular television host and model in Mexico City, was one of the many friends Ricky had made in the city. As the host of such illustrious events as Miss Universe and Supermodel of the World competition, Rebeca understood what it meant to be famous. Part of what attracted Ricky to her in the first place was that she wasn't impressed by his status. When the two first met at a discotheque, both felt an instant attraction. Unfortunately, Ricky couldn't be certain whether Rebeca was interested in friendship or romance.

Although he had plenty of girlfriends during Menudo, Ricky never learned how to develop a healthy and stable relationship. The fear of letting Rebeca down kept him from exposing his true intentions. Finally, he decided to throw caution to the wind. Their mutual attraction had become too strong to deny, and the pair was soon inseparable. For the first time, Ricky had fallen madly and deeply in love. He had come a long way from his former days as a playboy. "When I was younger, all the girls were after me because I was in a very popular band," he told *Salut*. "I took advantage of it a lot, then I realized it wouldn't get me anywhere. Since the age of nineteen, I looked for deeper and more stable relationships. I'm actually a great romantic. I believe in eternal love, the real thing, romance."

From Ricky's standpoint, Rebeca was the ideal girlfriend to tame his wild soul. An adventurous, high-spirited young woman, Rebeca's keen sense of humor and joie de vivre were just what Ricky needed. "For a woman to win my heart she must have something very simple—spontaneity," Ricky expressed to *El Norte Newspaper*. "I don't complicate my life. I am not look-

ing for beauty, for intelligence . . . What attracts me is
spontaneity, a girl who is not afraid to make a fool of
herself. Do you understand what I mean? She's fun.
She can be herself. She pampers herself. She knows
how to pamper others, there is absolutely no doubt
about that. She takes care of her skin, takes care of
herself, but, at the same time, has a very carefree personality.''

Rebeca and Ricky became one of Mexico's hottest
young couples. Their every move was recorded on film,
as paparazzi scrambled to get a shot of the beautiful
pair on their many outings to the theater, to nightclubs,
or to restaurants. The lack of privacy, however, was
beginning to take a toll on the young lovers. As a result, Ricky became very protective of his new relationship, adopting a strict policy about discussing his new
love interest. "Rebeca is someone very special," he
explained to *Jet Set.* "I understand that a gentleman
doesn't talk about his women and respect them. Why
make the person you go out with public?"

Meanwhile, Ricky's solo career was also taking time
away from the budding relationship. Upon completing
his debut album, *Ricky Martin*, he was required to take
off on a whirlwind round of promotional interviews,
music store appearances, and press junkets. The stress
of having to balance his personal and professional lives
was immense. Not only did he have to make time in
his schedule for Rebeca, she was also busy fulfilling
the demands of her own career. Luckily, their strong
love for one another united them even when they were
miles apart.

All in all, Ricky had little cause for complaint. When
news of his self-titled album broke, his ever-increasing
fan base was eager to sing its praises. It was a very
emotional time for the young artist. Not only had he

finally found the woman of his dreams, but his musical career was gaining momentum and a loyal following. Ricky could not believe that his first effort had been so successful. He was equally overcome when he heard his first single emanating from the radio. "Well, I need to be really honest," he confided in *Boxtalk*. "When I first heard my song on the radio, I cried. Men do cry."

A triumph throughout Mexico, the groundswell of support for the album demanded that Ricky go on tour. To prepare for his first-ever solo excursion through Latin America, he choreographed his dance moves, arranged for show-stopping special effects, and rehearsed for weeks with his backup band. Ricky made sure that his first solo tour would be one audiences would not soon forget. Although he was confident that he could provide his fans with a no-holds-barred spectacle, he was worried about selling enough tickets. He never suspected that his tour would sell out completely only a few short weeks after it had been announced. Hit singles such as "Fuego contra Fuego," "Dime que me Quieres," and "Susana" firmly established Ricky Martin as the hottest ticket in town. Life was good.

After completing a hectic touring schedule, Ricky's first album obtained gold status in Mexico, Chile, Argentina, Colombia, Puerto Rico, and the United States. Fans who had no idea who he was or where he'd come from were lining up by the thousands to meet the new singing sensation. And this time, Ricky knew how to handle the fame. Thanks to his early brush with mass adulation, he approached this second go-round with no small measure of equanimity. Eternally grateful to his innumerable supporters, he paid homage to his fans by personally signing as many autographs and posing for as many pictures as their hearts desired.

Ricky Martin sold a total of 500,000 copies through-

out the world, a number that established him as one of
Sony's top Latin debuts in the past decade. The album
also garnered many awards, including the Lo Nuestro
and Eres awards. Ricky Martin was well on his way to
conquering the music industry.

To follow up his first hit record, Ricky was quickly
ushered into the studio to begin work on his second
album, *Me Amarás* (*Will You Love Me?*). The year was
1992, and Ricky was more in love with Rebeca than
ever. She had proven her commitment and devotion by
standing by him throughout his tumultuous tour. Having passed this test of love, the couple's ardor and zest
for each other's company seemed only to increase with
time. On one particularly memorable occasion, the two
were having so much fun together that Ricky wound
up a no-show at his own concert. While this irrespon-
sible act was tantamount to treason in the eyes of the
many fans who'd gathered for the event, Ricky argued
that it was but a crime of passion. "I discovered that
love is the strongest thing when I missed a big concert
in Mexico; it was a Ricky Martin concert," he candidly
told *Salut*. "In fact, I was having such a good time
with the girl I loved at the time that I never went up
on stage. So I had to refund thousands of seats with
my own money. It was the craziest moment of my life,
and I'll never forget that unique experience!"

No amount of passion, however, could keep him
from the studio. The record company wanted to strike
while the iron was hot, and Ricky was under strict or-
ders to put out a new album. *Me Amarás* was even
more personal and romantic than his eponymous debut.
Ricky tried to include additional ballads to reflect his
contemplative and peaceful state of mind. Working

alongside acclaimed producer Juan Carlos Calderon, he found his second foray into the studio to be an even more rewarding experience than the first. By now, he was an old pro, and his increased comfort level was made apparent by the artistry and beauty of each song.

Me Amarás proved even more successful than his first album, selling over 700,000 copies through the world. Anxiously awaited by his fans, the sophomore effort managed to exceed the public's greatest expectations. The album soared to the top of the Latin charts, staying at the top week after week. During that year, Ricky was also invited to open the renowned Chile festival, Viña del Mar. The culmination of his success came with a Billboard award nomination for "Best Latin Artist" in 1993. Considering the mixed bag of reviews that had greeted both of his albums, the Billboard nod could not have come at a better time.

Yet the same middling reviews that had made the nomination so welcome were also responsible for Ricky's insecurity around awards time. While he always had recourse to the old "it's an honor just being nominated" cliché, he desperately wanted to come home a winner. Since he had some pretty stiff competition to contend with, Ricky was certain that he'd walk away empty-handed. So sure was he of his inevitable failure that he hadn't so much as prepared a speech. Of course, when the envelope was opened, it was Ricky's name that pierced the tense silence. Surprised and elated, he hurried to the podium, delivering an impassioned speech that came straight from his heart.

Having come to Mexico to make his mark only a few years ago, Ricky had all that he'd ever wanted. He had the girl, the fame, and the money. What more could any man ask for? He had made it.

Of course, for Ricky, "making it" did not entail putting in for early retirement. As he still had a lot of living to do, he worried about keeping his priorities straight and his music on track. This was no time to fall into complacency. With everyone from his publicists to his manager to his roadies stroking his ego and feeding him nothing but words of kindness, it would have been all too easy to get carried away by his considerable success. But Ricky knew that all the hype could hamper his perspective. Above all, he wanted to maintain integrity as an artist, something he wouldn't be able to do if his thinking was clouded with thoughts of his own greatness.

So after completing his second promotional tour for *Me Amarás*, Ricky decided to take a break from music altogether. Through his tenure with Menudo, he learned that overexposure could be the kiss of death for a talented artist. Since he had been a featured guest on countless television shows, appeared on dozens of magazine covers, and performed in many countries, Ricky knew that he was coming dangerously close to a public burnout. He was also tired from the constant performances and publicity-related events. A break from all the activity would come as a welcome relief. "I did a tour of Latin America, 120 concerts, then I returned to Mexico and recorded my second album," he explained to *Hitkrant*. "I toured again and then I decided to take another break so people wouldn't lose interest in me too fast."

While wrapping up his second tour through Latin America and Europe, Ricky began to see signs of trouble in his relationship with Rebeca. The rumor mill had it that while shopping for Rebeca's engagement ring, he got a sudden case of cold feet and bolted for the door. Perhaps it was this much-publicized occurrence that led to the couple's subsequent breakup. For no sooner had Ricky come home from his tour, than Rebeca told him that they were through.

The declaration came as a painful blow to Ricky's ego. She wanted a commitment, he wanted to take his time. Although he was still very much in love with Rebeca, the young man wasn't ready to settle down just yet. The loss still haunts him to this very day. "Now I'm single, I don't have anyone," he confessed to *El Norte Newspaper*. "But it is not something that I think about now. And if she comes along, honestly, it is a good time. I'm really happy, in the true sense of the word 'happy.' As a person alone, I'm fine. Look, I'm being sincere. I want to have a wife and I want to have a really big family, and I want to be a great father, and I want to give my family everything, and I want to see my grandchildren. Honestly, I would be a lost soul if I died without having the opportunity to be a father and raise a family. But, right now, that is not the case. I have my experiences. I'm human. Some experiences are fulfilling, others are not, but I keep moving on."

Wanting to put the pain of the breakup behind him, Ricky thought long and hard about his next move. Always looking for a new challenge, he decided to give acting another try. He had already established himself as a singer and performer, and acting seemed like the final frontier. And what better place to do that than in Hollywood. Tempted by the glitter and glamour of Tinseltown, he bought a one-way ticket to Los Angeles and began a new chapter of his life.

CHAPTER 4

California Dreaming

Millions of actors arrive in Los Angeles every year. Only a scant few make it to the upper echelons of movie stardom. Although he could hardly be considered a nobody in the entertainment industry, Ricky had never worked as a professional actor in the United States. If he wanted to find a reputable agent and book auditions, he would have to work just as hard as anybody else.

It was just like Ricky to humble himself while at the peak of his musical career. Nothing got his juices flowing quite like reality. One of the most celebrated personalities in Mexico City, he was content with pounding the pavement with the rest of Hollywood's many wannabes. "Most important to me is to keep my feet on the ground," he confirmed to *Diversion*. "Humility has taken me to where I am."

His first step toward establishing himself as an actor was finding an agent. After speaking with several prospective representatives, Ricky found someone who was willing to go out on the line for him each and every day. It was only a couple of weeks before he was being sent out on auditions. Unfortunately, the market for Latino actors was smaller than he had expected. He did, however, appear in several episodes of *Getting By*, an NBC sitcom that ran for a total of eighteen months. Although the experience wouldn't catapult his star very far, he was happy to get the professional credit on his resume. But even while his agent along with his personal manager, Jose Luis Vega, worked overtime to procure a role that would complement Ricky's style and abilities, the right part would be long in the coming.

During this rather stressful and uncertain time, Ricky kept himself busy by decorating his new house in the Hollywood Hills and taking care of his new dog, Icaro, a golden retriever. He enjoyed the anonymity of being in Los Angeles. In Mexico City, Ricky couldn't go anywhere without having to sign autographs and pose for photos. The paparazzi followed him day and night. The return to solitude was one of the most pleasant aspects of moving to LA.

But Ricky couldn't isolate himself forever. To alleviate his boredom, he soon found a roommate who became one of his closest friends to date. The two were inseparable. They would eat together, shop together, and go out together. Having a friend in a strange, new city worked wonders for Ricky's outlook. "I like the American kind of life. When I'm at home in Los Angeles, I can go to the supermarket in peace. I buy tons of stuff that I put in my car and bring home," he conveyed to *Salut*. "Then, my roommate cooks nice little meals while I'm out walking my dog. I'm a pretty bad cook, so I prefer to let him do that."

One night, while enjoying a relaxing evening in front of the TV, Ricky received a call from his agent. Apparently, America's highest-rated soap opera, *General Hospital*, was looking for a young Latino actor to join its illustrious cast. They had been searching unsuccessfully for months, until Ricky's agent sent in his concert tapes. After watching him perform on stage, the producers were anxious to get Ricky in for an audition. Wendy Riche, executive producer of *General Hospital*, explained to *People*, "Our head writer saw the tapes [of Martin in concert] and said, 'Wow! If he can act, let's sign him up.'"

With his stomach tied into nervous knots, Ricky entered the screening room and read in front of a large group of series regulars, producers, and casting directors. He had no idea what to expect. Although he had acted before, Spanish soap operas were very different from their U.S. counterparts. "If there is a reason we Hispanics watch a soap, it is to see the end of it," he elucidated to *Hitkrant*. "I have never thought of this before. I do not think we care about watching a soap for thirty-three years. In the U.S. it is different. *General Hospital* is an institution, but we just like our soaps to last six months and then watch another one."

For all his agitation, Ricky still managed to impress everyone in the room. A natural in front of the camera, he delivered his lines with precision and grace. After being asked to wait for five minutes, he was offered the role of Miguel Morez. This was just the break he had been looking for. "I really wanted to do something on American TV and they were looking for a Spanish-speaking guy who could sing and act," he told *Hitkrant*. "They found me; I did an audition and that was it."

As excited as he was to have won the role, Ricky was too smart to accept the offer without first learning about the character he would be playing. The fact that Miguel was a singer from Puerto Rico was about the extent of his knowledge on the subject. Before he could finalize the deal, he had to make sure that the role would not perpetuate any negative stereotypes about the Puerto Rican people. His decision to act in the United States was partly based on his desire to provide a positive role model for Latinos. "When it comes to being Latin, it's not as bad as saying that we are all the equivalent of *West Side Story*—with the gangs, the mafia, the cocaine and stuff," he asserted to *Cleo*. "So, given a choice, I guess it's better to be known as a lover than a fighter. I'm very proud of my culture and I understand that stereotypes come from ignorance. The best way to change minds is to teach people."

That's why it was especially important for Ricky to have input where his character was concerned. Fortunately, Miguel Morez was as noble and dignified as the actor chosen to portray him. Miguel was written in as a former singer from Puerto Rico, who arrives in the fictional town of Port Charles to study natural science and escape his past as a popular musician. To support his studies, Miguel works as an orderly in General Hospital by day and a bartender by night. At first, little is revealed about the mysterious lothario in hospital scrubs.

In June of 1994, however, the audience discovered that Miguel had been hiding his successful career as a musician. When he meets Julio Iglesias in New York City, the truth about the deliberate stranger is finally disclosed. "Miguel has a lot of secrets, and one of them is that he used to be a singer in Puerto Rico. That's where Julio Iglesias comes in," he told *Hispanic* magazine. "He encourages me to go back to my singing career in spite of the past."

The plot line drew heavily upon Ricky's own experiences. In real life, the actor was just as big an admirer of Julio Iglesias as was Miguel. In a statement to *TV Week*, Ricky talked about the influence that the mu-

sical legend has had on his own life: "He's my godfather in music. I have been able to work with him and
he's given me many words of wisdom. I really do admire him. But I don't want to be him, I want to follow
in his steps, if you know what I mean. He is a very
wise man."

Because Ricky's life experience was so similar to
Miguel's, the writers and producers often consulted
with Ricky before planning the episodes. For instance,
like Ricky, Miguel sent money to his family in Puerto
Rico. Another parallel had to do with the fact that Miguel, like Ricky, left his home when he lost his true
love. The insight he gained into Miguel's character,
helped Ricky craft a realistic and sensitive portrayal.
"He's passionate toward everything—music, school,
friends—and he hates injustice," he said of Miguel.
Sound vaguely familiar?

On the show, the advice of his mentor gave Miguel
the courage to return to his roots as a singer. Eventually, Miguel signed a recording contract with L&B
Records, and reconciled with his old flame, Lily. Re-
viving Miguel's musical past was especially rewarding.
It was the first time that he could showcase his skills
in front of a large American audience. He took every
opportunity to sing on the small screen. By combining
singing and acting like in his days on the Spanish soap
opera, Ricky was, once again, having his cake and eating it too. He asserted to *Latin Music Online*, "I think
the soap fed the music career, and the music fed the
acting, like a circular process."

While many critics lambasted Ricky for abandoning
his solo career, he believed that following one activity
didn't necessarily preclude his pursuing the other. In
his opinion, well-honed acting skills would actually im-
prove his overall stage presence and delivery. "For me,

General Hospital has been an incredible way of learning and growing as an actor," he told *Hispanic* magazine. "I look at it as a training school that's going to help my acting career. I think this will even help me in my musical career. At concerts, I'm always in front of the public, and acting gives you more self-confidence."

What made his time on *General Hospital* even more memorable were the bonds he forged with the cast. Whether it was attending a birthday party or hanging out after a long day's work, Ricky was always the first one invited. His sense of humor and fun anecdotes about his past kept everyone glued to their seats. He made such a good impression on the cast, that many of them still keep in touch with him today.

Besides winning over the series regulars, Ricky found a place in the heart of American fans. Viewers swooned over the well-built, long-haired Romeo that looked as if he just stepped off a romance novel cover. He was just the kind of actor to put the simmer in daytime television. During his fifteen-month run with the show, Ricky received thousands of letters from fans, letters that often included phone numbers, provocative photographs, and proposals of marriage. "The mail response on him is very positive," executive producer Wendy Riche confirmed to *People*. "Ricky will be very big."

Indeed, the demand for Ricky had become so great that he was called upon to give interviews and appear on talk shows. Ever since his maiden episode in February, 1994, he had become one of the most popular actors on the show. Once the news spread about the latest addition to the *General Hospital* staff, Ricky found himself in the awkward position of having to turn down offers. He did, however, make the time to appear in such popular magazines and television shows as *People*, *YM*, *Seventeen*, *The Oprah Winfrey Show*, *Entertainment Tonight*, *Good Morning America*, *Live with Regis and Kathy Lee*, *The Ricki Lake Show*, and *Extra*. Ricky was the toast of the country. In one master stroke, he had won acclaim both for his acting and his singing. More important, he accomplished what he'd set out to do—present a positive role model for Latino viewers.

Though he had little cause for complaint, Ricky was not entirely satisfied with his life. No matter how much success he achieved or how much money he amassed, he couldn't seem to shake the nagging pain in his heart. Since 1985, Ricky hadn't spoken with his father. So long as he didn't dwell on the matter too much, the estrangement didn't bother him. Yet, being alone in Los Angeles provided him with the one thing he didn't want—the opportunity to reflect upon the past. "In a very intense year for me, when I was fetching for a reconciliation with my father, a year that I was quite unstable in Los Angeles and I had a lot of time to be with myself," he recounted, "I went to the mountain and cried if I had to cry, and I broke this necessity of always being accompanied, of entering a house and, if I was alone, just turning on the television. And then came the tears, the anxiety attack, and these really helped me to think and to put the things in their right places."

The time of quiet reflection revealed that the argument with his father had had severe ramifications on his state of mind and well-being. He was shocked to discover that he had changed dramatically over the years, and not for the better. "While I was away from my father, I became a cynic," he told the *Los Angeles Times*. "I was cold, sarcastic; I didn't like children. I was a different person. Now, I'm dying to be a father. I actually have more of a desire to be a dad than a husband.''

To mend the wound that he'd left untreated for so many years, Ricky finally broke down and called his father, Enrique. The decision was one of the hardest of his life, albeit not quite as difficult as choosing between his mom and his dad, as his father would have had him do nearly a decade prior. His pride had prevented him from reaching out to Enrique before, and even though he was still upset about his father's past behavior, he wanted to let bygones be bygones. Life was too short to be spent in harboring a grudge, especially at Christmas.

"At the end of 1993, it was a very special time period in my life because I hadn't seen my dad in years and it was tearing me apart," he told *Salut*. "After I left Puerto Rico, he had a fight with my mom and they hurt each other a lot and they hurt me at the same time. I had a lot against my father at the time. On December 24, 1993, I was depressed and I couldn't stop thinking about him. I called him and we made up. It was like taking a huge weight off my back."

Once the air had been cleared, Ricky and Enrique were as close as ever. They spent hours on the phone, catching up on everything they had missed out on. Ricky was pleased to learn that although they had not had contact in years, his father had been following his career closely. Secretly, Enrique's heart swelled with pride at the thought of his son's many successes. And while he tried not to let on, he longed for a reconciliation every bit as much as Ricky did. Scared that his son would never forgive him, he decided to let Ricky make the first move. And once he did, it was like nothing had ever happened.

The peace treaty between father and son had an incredible impact on Ricky's life. For a long time, Ricky had been sullen, depressed, and unwilling to face his inner demons. After the dispute had been settled, he was, by all accounts, a new man. His coworkers, like Lilly Melgar (Lily Rivera) were stunned by the sudden transformation. "After he reconciled with his father, Ricky's been the happiest I've ever seen him," she told *People*. "He has inner peace."

The evil spell that seemed to have been cast over Ricky's life had lifted in a snap. He now felt carefree, clearheaded, and ready to express all the tears that had been welling up inside him for years. The need to expel his overwhelming emotion was what finally propelled him into the studio to record his third album, *A Medio Vivir* (Living Halfway).

A monumental undertaking, the album was a revolutionary effort to redefine his musical and artistic boundaries. With its seamless fusion of pop, rock, and Latin rhythms, *A Medio Vevir* was to be symbolic of Ricky's rebirth into a mature and sophisticated performer. He was determined to craft an "alternative" album that would meld traditional Latin influences with a rock and roll attitude. It was as if Ricky's recent reconciliation with his father had taught him the true meaning of being an artist; someone who wasn't afraid to take chances and go out on a limb for the sake of his work. "It was very important for me to do this kind of music because it helps me to break boundaries," he asserted to *Latin Music Online*. "That's what I want, that's what I need to do."

Wishing to make a significant contribution to the album that would bear his name, Ricky felt it incumbent upon him to write and produce. Because he was

still with *General Hospital*, he relied on his spare time
and stolen moments to facilitate the creative process.
In order to write from the heart, he needed to find a
serene place, devoid of all distractions, where he could
be alone with his thoughts. "It's exciting to move to a
new place and to discover a new culture," he told
Salut. "It's a great source of inspiration for a song-
writer. When I write, I need a change of environment,
of atmosphere. In Los Angeles, you can leave the city
to find yourself in the desert, or near the ocean. And
don't forget the earthquakes! That's where I've recorded my new album, in a studio surrounded by little
hills. It's a very peaceful place and I had a very nice
experience."

Ricky's decision to set up a studio on the outskirts
of town was a sound one. By recording in LA, he could
simultaneously fulfill the obligations of his demanding
acting and musical careers. While the CD would take
up to a year to complete, Ricky saw no reason to rush
the production. The desire to craft a unique and wholly
original album led Ricky to scour the world for the
most talented producers. Securing the production ex-
pertise of K.C. Porter and Robi Rosa was an immense
coup. Responsible for arranging albums for such artists
as Bon Jovi, Richard Marx, Selena, Patti LaBelle, and
Los Fabulosos Cadillacs, Porter was a constant source
of inspiration for Ricky. He had also been instrumental
in translating into Spanish the hits of such popular musical acts as Boyz II Men and Janet Jackson.

Robi Rosa was an equally important factor in the
album's creation. A former member of Menudo, Rosa
had developed a reputation as one of the leading singers
and producers in the Latin music industry. Ricky's respect for Rosa was considerable. He had no trouble
recognizing talent, and considered Rosa's to be one of

the most brilliant musical minds in history.

"I think [Rosa is] a genius," he enthused to *Latin Music Online*. "From the age of twelve he was always in front of the piano, I remember him. He just recorded his second album, I heard it and it's poetry, it's deep poetry. His favorite poet is Arthur Rimbaud. Musically, he has incredible taste. I mean, you can ask him: 'Robi, let's do something dark, let's do something like "Maria,'" boom, "'Let's do something classical like the bridge from "Volverás,'" . . . and that's him. He deserves a lot more credit, but you see at the same time he doesn't do his music for credit, he does his music for himself. He just loves being in the studio and just creating. In the long run, in five, six, ten years from now, Robi's going to get all the credit he deserves . . . Oh, I talk about him everywhere, everywhere. When people ask me, I tell them that I'm very proud to be working with him. He has so much to give."

The collaboration enjoyed by Ricky and the production team, including Franco DeVita, Alejandro Sanz, Cristóbal Sansano, Mónica Naranjo, Marcos Flores, Luis Gomez Escolar, Carlos Lara, Luis Angel, and Manolo Tena, freed him emotionally and artistically. Although Ricky had played an important role on the production of his first two albums, those experiences weren't nearly as gratifying as the making of *A Medio Vevir*. Pervading the studio was a natural give and take that allowed all the players to put forth their best work. Ricky was also grateful for the effort each artist made to translate his personal experiences into beautiful compositions. "I sat with different composers and told them what I wanted to express; what I was going through at that moment of my life and how I wanted to approach the audience with that album," he told *Latin Music Online*. "Franco DeVita, Alejandro Sanz,

Louis Gomez Escolar, who I think is a genius, a poet! I want to keep working with them forever.''

The camaraderie in the studio created an atmosphere that fostered creativity and experimentation. Ricky recalls that time as one of the most liberating of his life. Members of the production team would often stage informal jam sessions that would last until the early morning hours. While the public may have viewed these Latin artists as each other's rivals, all vying for the same audience, the group that had assembled for the making of *A Medio Vevir* had come together for one purpose alone—to make music history. So involved and captivated by the process were they that the line between work and having fun became blurrier with every meeting. ''Franco DeVita, Carlos Lara, a great Mexican friend. Many people tell me that they are my competition but they are not,'' Ricky told *La Entrevista*. ''We are just young guys who want to explore our talents and take it everywhere.''

Ricky's insight into his past provided the composers with ample fuel for their creative journey. As a result, every song and every lyric has personal meaning for Ricky. By making sense of his sometimes scattered and disorganized thoughts, Ricky recognized how much room there was for personal growth. ''I have so much to learn! I've been in this business for ten years but I have a hell of a lot to learn,'' he said. ''I have a lot to learn about myself, about realizing how great it is to be alone for a little while. Just putting my thoughts in order and finding out how to express my experiences. How to share them with the audience. I have a lot of things to talk about.''

Despite the fact that so many hands had a part in the making of *A Medio Vevir*, Ricky's voice would be the one to resonate throughout the globe. By taking his time, he was finally able to organize his thoughts and express his innermost sentiments to the world. And although he only wrote one album track, "Volveras," each song provided an honest reflection of his individual strength and personal beliefs. Even the title, *A Medio Vevir*, was a way to illuminate his new perspective to his fans.

"I named it like that because I think that it is the way we humans are living life right now, we are living half of it," Ricky revealed to *La Entrevista*. "A lot of people tell me I am negative if I see it that way, but I think I am realistic. I wake up and read the many problems in the paper, and if I have the chance to send a message in my songs and express it to the public, why not? We humans worry more about talking about our neighbors than loving them . . . It is time to start loving each and that is in my music. It is a 'Hello . . . Wake Up!' "

Once the album was completed, Ricky couldn't help feeling like a proud father. Each song was like his own child, a living, breathing thing born of his soul, hard work, and wisdom. He still feels extremely attached to each song. Recently, while describing the emotion that gave birth to the track, "Te Extrano, Te Olvido, Te Amo," he appeared visibly moved by the recollection. "It is a story full of contradictions. It means, 'I miss you, I forgive you, and I love you,' " he conveyed to *Salut*. "It is about the highs and lows that you go through after a love story. You know when a love story ends, you go through several stages that are so different that you have a hard time knowing where you are. And because that happened to me, I tried to apply in words what I was feeling, and that is where the single came from."

Another song that was close to his heart was the

smash hit "Maria." One of the most widely played
tracks from the album, "Maria" spoke about a femme
fatale who toys with men's hearts with reckless abandon. "It is the rhythms that are not so well-known,"
Ricky indicated to *Gala*. "That's why. The mixture
between Flamenco, Caribbean, and Brazilian sounds.
All that made the song something special."

Yet, while the rhythms may have steered the club
hoppers' feet toward the dance floors, it was the tale
of love lost that touched their lonely souls. Many began
to speculate about Maria's identity. Was she a woman
from Ricky's past or just a figment of his blessed imagination? Inquiring minds wanted to know.

Ricky, meanwhile, was tiring of the obtrusive que-
ries. After being asked "Who is Maria?" for the hun-
dredth time, Ricky grew exasperated and decided to put
an end to the mystery. But instead of telling the public
exactly what they wanted to hear, he used humorous
subterfuge to quell the tide of curiosity miring him at
every turn. "She was a very intense computer program," he half-joked with *Cleo*. "I wanted to get
closer to my roots, to my culture. We started digging
around, looking for sounds and rhythms on the computer and that's how it came about—it wasn't any spe-
cific girl. I mean, Maria could be anyone—even
someone's dog. It's not about someone special. I can
be very romantic—stupidly romantic, actually—but not
in this case."

Even if the album hadn't broken all of Ricky's prior
records, he would have been just as satisfied with the
achievement it represented. As luck would have it,
however, the September, 1995 release of *A Medio Vevir*
brought great acclaim to the singer. The album was met
with considerable critical and commercial success.

While the layman and -woman had long been receptive to his verse, he had always yearned for those elusive rave reviews. Ricky was relieved to learn that the album found favor with the critics. *A Medio Vevir* was, after all, a succession of calculated artistic risks. Just knowing that they had paid off smoothed out the kinks in the young artist's frazzled nerves.

After spending many grueling months in the studio, the last thing he wanted to think about was going on tour. Traveling would require an immense expenditure of energy, the one thing that Ricky couldn't afford to spare. Yet his manager and publicist were all focused on the bottom line. Ricky's public was clamoring for his return. And where there was a need, there was money to be made. Ricky, however, wanted to remain focused on the spirituality that had helped him complete the album. He feared that venturing out on a multicountry tour would only harden him, reversing all the emotional strides he had made in the past year.

While he was pondering the course of his own self-realization, his fans were demanding their due share of attention. When the first single "Te Extrano, Te Olvido, Te Amo" was released, it was obvious that the masses would not rest until they had seen Ricky in the flesh. The situation became even more aggravated when the single "Maria" hit the stores. They had spent their hard-earned money on the CD, they'd memorized the words to every song, and now they wanted to dance to the live music. Ricky basically had no choice. He would have to return to his homeland.

As he was still a regular on *General Hospital*, he had to make advance arrangements with the show's producers. While the cast and crew loathed to part company with Ricky, they understood the claims of fame. The producers were happy to accommodate their resident sex symbol. He would be written out for a while, until he returned from his tour through Central and South America. Titled *Fuego de Noche Nieve de Día*, the tour would begin in Puerto Rico and then take him through Mexico and all of Spain.

Once Ricky had reconciled himself to the necessity of touring, he was consumed by tremendous agitation. Having spread his music throughout Latin America before, the veteran crooner was not expected to entertain any self-doubts this time around. Yet Ricky was not the same cocksure buck who, just two years ago, could ascend the stage without a moment's hesitation. The making of *A Medio Vivir* had altered the very fiber of his constitution, and he was apprehensive that his old friends and fans would not readily accept his new, improved, and more introspective self.

Fortunately, the sleepless nights Ricky had spent while racked with worry were all for naught. The reception he received was nothing if not warm. Anticipation for his arrival had been mounting for several weeks, and by the time he actually alighted in Puerto Rico, the locals could talk of little else. Once again, distance had proven no match for the love of his loyal following. Having accustomed himself to the blasé ways of Los Angeles, Ricky was nearly lulled into a false sense of anonymity. He never foresaw the wild reaction awaiting him and his music in Puerto Rico. In a matter of days, he had effectively bridged the great divide separating minor celebrities from awe-inducing superstars.

While he'd been working diligently in the studio, Ricky had not given the album's commercial success, or lack thereof, much thought. As long as he was becoming a better and more talented person every day, money didn't matter. Yet when the album began selling out like gangbusters, Ricky couldn't deny the joy in his heart. "Maybe I knew it would do well, but I'm trying to be humble about it," he offered to *Latin Music Online*. "Because what you have today may not be with you tomorrow. And if you want it to stay, then you have to work at it."

Ricky had made good on his promise to himself. The strength, hope, and courage with which he'd invested the album were now paying dividends of a material as well as an emotional nature. At long last, he could look at the fruit of his labor and join the fans in their vociferous approbation. The record was his most honest and personal work to date, and the bravery he'd shown in making it was not lost on anyone, least of all on Ricky himself. He was proud, not only of his album, but of the many obstacles he'd had to surpass in order to arrive at his spiritual and emotional awakening. ". . . I was satisfied. There are many experiences in this CD and I hope you enjoy them," he apprised *La Entrevista*. "It is part of my life."

CHAPTER 5

Bright Light on Broadway

During the last leg of the *Fuego de Noche Nieve de Día* tour, Ricky was gripped by a sense of urgency. He was getting older and felt obligated to plan out the next segment of his life. A return to *General Hospital* seemed unavoidable. The producers expected his arrival any day, structuring the plot to reflect his entry. What they hadn't expected, however, was that Ricky would grow tired of playing Miguel day in and day out. The monotony entailed in working on a daytime drama had not bothered Ricky at first. But now that he'd become reacquainted with the life of a jet-setter, he couldn't go back to his old routine.

When he first arrived on the set, Ricky tried to hide his change of heart. Everyone was so happy to see him, he couldn't let them down by quitting right then and there. He continued this charade for several months. Although he had decided to leave the soap, Ricky still had no definite plans for the future. He had grown tired of touring, and couldn't fathom going back to the recording studio so soon after he had completed *A Medio Vivir*. Reinvigorating his acting career seemed like the most tempting option. Only by portraying a variety of roles could he rediscover the thrill of his craft and stretch his thespian muscles. As he was still a permanent fixture on *General Hospital*, keeping his job search a secret from the show's producers and actors became a top priority. Since they had become like a family to him, Ricky felt guilty about leaving them in the lurch.

During his surreptitious quest for a new role, Ricky stumbled upon several opportunities, one of which was a role in the a television pilot tentatively titled *Barefoot in Paradise*. Since thousands of qualified actors had been up for the part that had gone to Ricky, his selection as one of the stars of the pilot was a considerable achievement in its own right. Geared for prime time, the pilot could have provided him with an even greater measure of exposure in the United States. Alas, after completing his work on the pilot episode, it failed to be picked up by a network.

Just like any actor who is picked for a pilot, Ricky was excited by the idea of headlining a series. But, surprisingly enough, he was not disappointed with the final verdict. In fact, he understood why the networks passed on the project first-hand. "The story was horrible," he explained to America Online. "But Zalman King did a great job as a director. That was to our benefit."

For Ricky, the show's ultimate failure was nothing short of a narrow escape. Although he'd put a lot of effort into bringing his character to life, that was nothing compared to the late hours he'd have to keep if the pilot was bought by a network. Considering the low quality of the project, the chances of him finding much joy in his work were slim to none. Anyway, Ricky knew that time was the only thing standing between him and the opportunity he had been waiting for.

When parceling through scripts, Ricky relied on artistic integrity as his sole guideline. The right project was out there, unfortunately, it was as difficult to find as a needle in a haystack. When the producers of the syndicated hit *Baywatch* wanted Ricky to sign on as a regular, he balked at the offer. With Ricky's international following and *Baywatch*'s multicultural appeal, the combination might have scored big for all involved. However, the show's vapid writing style and minimalist dress code offended his finer sensibilities, and Ricky wasn't biting.

He had worked very hard to prove that he was much more than a pretty face. In the process, his mission to be judged on the basis of his talent as opposed to his stunning good looks had gained even greater importance. He wasn't about to undo years of effort just to get on a TV show. Shedding his pretty-boy image was just too important. When asked how his status as a teen idol affected him professionally, he had this to say to the *New York Daily News*: "I'm working hard to get rid of that. Eventually, that [image] will vanish a little, so it doesn't bother me. I just want a long and steady career in music and acting and to still be doing this in thirty years. If it takes me forever to get there, that's good—as long as it lasts."

While his fellow actors chastised him for not jumping on the *Baywatch* bandwagon, he was determined to follow his heart. Turning down offers of regular acting work was a luxury, to be sure. Most actors stage a party if so much as a commercial comes their way, and Ricky knew it. "I am one of those people who fights hard for the public to demand more from artists, and sometimes the material that you are given is not defensible in that aspect," he explained. "That is why I refuse to do things I don't believe in, although I should say that I have been fortunate, because I have not had the economic necessity to do anything that I don't like."

After making gigantic strides in the artistic community with his third album, *A Medio Vevir*, he could not take his credibility for granted. No amount of money or exposure was worth losing his life's work, his good reputation. Having broken with *General Hospital* for purposes of creative freedom, Ricky could not bring himself to sign up with *Baywatch*.

Luckily, just as he was mulling over the *Baywatch* offer, a producer of Broadway's acclaimed production of *Les Miserables* came looking for him. Sensing that joining in the production could enhance his career, Ricky was thrilled with the offer. The Great White Way had been his dream for years, ever since he'd had a chance to live in the city as a teen. "The producers of *Baywatch* wanted me to be in the series. But I said no because at the same time I was about to get a role in *Les Miserables*," he told *Star Club*. "To me, theater is more important than TV, it gives you credibility that TV series or films will never give you."

Steeped in the theatrical tradition, the word "Broadway" conjures up a distinguished array of imagery. Thousands hark to the call of the New York stage every year, and Ricky was eager to join them. "When I was in Miami, a journalist asked me, 'What do you still have to do to be able to die a happy man?' And I said, 'I just have to play Broadway once, in a theater in New York.' And believe it or not, one of those Broadway producers read that article! So he called me and simply offered me a role in *Les Miserables*! I was yelling again of course. 'Um . . . well, send me some material and I'll see if I can fit it into my schedule.' "

After a quick meeting with the famed producer Richard Jay-Alexander, Ricky began making arrangements for his special limited engagement with *Les Miserables*. Of course, before he could depart for New York, he would have to say goodbye to his *General Hospital* pals. After announcing his plans to make it big on Broadway, Ricky was surprised to find a marked lack of hard feelings on the set. Everyone was proud of him and wished him the best of luck on his next journey. While he had expected his character to be written out of the show via a death scene, no such repercussions were forthcoming. The producers actually left the door wide open should Ricky ever wish to return. "Thank God they didn't kill me," he breathed a sigh of relief during a *Latin Music Online* interview. "So, I can come back. And even if they did kill me I could still come back because they also do that a lot. But not for now, now I need to give some time for music, and for the next level, Broadway."

Leaving his friends at *General Hospital* on such short notice could not keep Ricky from reflecting upon the show's impact on his career. Working in front of a camera every day, he had elevated his acting skills and sharpened his instincts. He was more polished, more professional, and more disciplined than ever before. *General Hospital* had been a stepping stone to bigger things, and Ricky would always be grateful for the time he spent playing Miguel. He was a better actor for the experience.

Gratitude aside, the chance to perform on Broadway was his real ticket to the top. In fact, for Ricky, Broadway *was* the top. He had paid his dues, and was now ready to experience everything the theater world had to offer. "Who could complain about having spent an hour a day for three years on American television? To introduce myself and become known, it was good. Even today, not being on the show, I meet people on the street who ask me when I will return. I don't believe that I'll do it. I think that, modesty aside, I am at

another level. I have made it to Broadway, which is
something so lovely. I have made a quantum leap.''

A favorite from Ricky Martin's own childhood, *Les
Miserables* has captivated the minds and hearts of millions of people over the years. Combining love, passion, and war into one unforgettable musical
experience, *Les Miserables* consistently ranks among
the most popular shows on Broadway.

Based on Victor Hugo's novel of the same name,
the story of *Les Miserables* opens in 1815 in the town
of Digne, France. Having served out a nineteen-year
prison term, Jean Valjean, a lowly commoner, is finally
being released. Ricky's character doesn't turn up until
the second half of the play. He played Marius, a young
man of lofty ideals and great privilege who joins forces
with the French Revolution. But after meeting and falling in love with Cosette, the daughter of protagonist
Jean Valjean, Marius must choose between his country
and his love for Cosette. The eruption of war separates
the passionate couple, but in the end Marius and Cosette are at last reunited.

Playing a romantic lead in this well-known period
piece was very appealing to Ricky. Like Marius, he
considered himself to be hot-blooded and courageous,
willing to drop everything to fight for a noble cause.
But unlike his character, Ricky had never had to struggle to survive. Marius's sympathetic plight intrigued
him from the start. ''Marius is very naive,'' he told
Soap Opera Weekly. ''But he's also been through a lot
of stuff that nobody knows about. There is a lot of
information in the Victor Hugo novel that isn't in the
script, so reading the book was like doing homework.
The character goes through a lot of changes. He's a
rich kid from the suburbs, and he goes to the city and

all of a sudden he's dying of hunger. Then his friend dies in his arms, and he meets some great guys who become his friends, but they all die too.''

After reviewing the script along with the book, Ricky was anxious to get started. It seemed that his entire life had been leading up to this one exciting event. ''It's definitely going to a new level in my career, and I've been getting ready for this for a long time,'' Ricky told the *New York Daily News*. ''I've been studying acting, and I've had the opportunity to do theater in Mexico to grow as an actor and singer. Broadway has always been my dream.''

Fearful of tarnishing his reputation as a consummate professional, Ricky wanted to be ready for his Broadway debut. Although his touring schedule was tight, he sat through *Les Miserables* twenty-seven times before even flying to New York. Studying the different depictions of Marius through the ages, Ricky was determined to excel in his Broadway debut. ''I wanted to make sure I got it right,'' he explained to *Soap Opera Magazine*. ''I'm on stage for nearly three hours because for the first fifty minutes I play a series of characters—a convict, a policeman, and a farmer—before I come on as Marius. In the theater, there's lighting, moving, singing, and dancing to worry about, and I wanted to do my homework.''

He simply couldn't afford to be sloppy. Realizing that his interpretation would get serious critical scrutiny, he was determined not to disappoint his fans. Although many actors-turned-singers, and vice versa, go on to have successful careers after a flop, Ricky understood himself well enough to know that he could not recover so easily from a failure. ''Whatever I'm doing in acting has a lot do with my music,'' he asserted to *Latin Music Online*. ''I'm doing *Les Miser-*

ables, which is something very important for me also. It's going to ask a lot from me as an actor and of course as a singer. I think that's going to be the perfect bridge for me from music to acting and acting to the next album.''

Although he considered *Les Miserables* an ideal transition into his fourth album, Ricky was completely focused on the task at hand. Despite his best efforts, the circumstances surrounding his first Broadway performance conspired to make his job even harder. Ricky, as it turned out, only had eleven days to rehearse with the theater company before the big night. In theater circles, an eleven-day rehearsal period for a new cast member was simply unheard of, but Ricky's touring schedule made anything more impossible. His crash course introduction to *Les Mise* was absolutely incomprehensible to his fellow actors. Frankly, they were curious to see if he could pull it off. ''I went to New York to rehearse the play for six days, then I took off for Spain to do some promotional concerts for my album, *A Medio Vivir*, then I came back to New York for four more days of rehearsal,'' he outlined his hectic itinerary to *Soap Opera Magazine*.

While his manager and friends urged him to cancel some shows and spare himself the humiliation, Ricky wouldn't hear of it. Always industrious, he wanted to complete his tour while rehearsing the role of Marius. He had never been so busy, and looked at the challenge as a way of testing the limits of his own endurance. But no matter how far he pushed himself, Ricky was no superhero. The strain of traveling, touring, and rehearsing took its toll on the all-too-human entertainer. No sooner had he returned from his last concert in Spain than he was diagnosed with a serious case of laryngitis. The doctor prohibited him from singing.

Ricky panicked. With only a few days left before his first performance on Broadway, he was forced to stay in bed and recuperate. As things stood, he had insufficient time for rehearsal, and would now have to try and wing it in front of a tough New York audience. Although he was legitimately scared by the new circumstances, the nail-biting experience taught Ricky an important lesson; it taught him the importance of self-preservation. "Imagine four or five days before your Broadway debut and your voice isn't functioning," he recalled. "I think it was probably due to the stress of flying back and forth and rehearsing from nine A.M. to midnight each day. I had to stop talking and rest."

No one should have to make their Broadway debut with swollen vocal chords and butterflies in their stomach, but that's precisely what Ricky had to do on opening night. To alleviate the tension and calm his frazzled nerves, Ricky turned to yoga and meditation. Little did he know, but everyone was just as nervous as he was. Since a play is only as strong as its weakest principal actor, the other players relied on Ricky to nail his dance steps and not miss any cues. One mistake could mean the difference between a standing ovation and general disapproval. Seeing that the rookie was anxious enough, the cast and crew tried to hide their feelings of doubt in order to help him relax.

Adding to the stress of the evening was the fact that Ricky's grandmother, who hates to fly, decided to come out to New York city in support of her beloved grandson. This was her first time in the United States, and Ricky worried about meeting her high expectations. For weeks, his grandmother had done little else but talk about Ricky's performance in *Les Miserables*. The pressure was mounting on all sides. "We were all calling this a historical occasion because my grandmother hates to fly,'' Ricky explained to *Soap Opera Magazine*. ''The last time she got on a plane was forty years ago, but she said to me, 'Since I don't get to see you on *General Hospital* every day now, I have to come see you in person'—and I'm so glad she did.''

Also in attendance that evening were both of Ricky's parents who had come straight from the airport. Some old friends from *General Hospital* showed up as well. Everyone had come out to see Ricky take charge of the Broadway stage.

When the lights finally dimmed and the audience grew silent, Ricky held his breath with anticipation. He had been so elated with the prospect of working on Broadway that he'd lost sight of the fact that he might not be ready to take on this challenge. Waiting in the wings, Ricky forgot the majority of what he had learned, everything from his name to his first line escaped him. The temporary loss of consciousness, however, was just that, temporary, because as soon he took to the stage he had regained enough composure to deliver all his lines and sing all his solos. ''I was scared to death,'' Ricky admitted. ''Every single scene, from the beginning to the end, I was just dying because the entire theater world was sitting there watching me. Thank God everyone said to me afterward, 'Oh, you looked so comfortable up there,' because I certainly didn't feel it.''

Performing live in front of large audiences had become second nature for Ricky. Instead of becoming meek in front of his fans, Ricky would always get a jolt of energy from the presence of so many smiling faces. But Broadway was a whole different matter. The audience members didn't know who he was, and were skeptical of the new kid on the block. ''I felt my adrenaline pumping because the audience that goes to my concerts is already convinced [of my talent]," he confided in *Soap Opera Magazine*, "but in the theater I still have to convince them. It was a real challenge."

Ricky was in rare form that night. While some performers buckle under pressure, he thrived in the spotlight. Despite his unwavering panic, he was thoroughly caught up in the magic of the evening. Not even the fear of an angry mob, or biting theater reviews for that matter, could shake his onstage composure. The vitality of the music and the lyrics overpowered him to such an extent that, for a brief moment, he actually thought he saw the cannons going off and soldiers fighting for *liberté*, *egalité*, and *fraternité*.

The finishing touch to the magical evening came in the form of his grandmother's delight and the cast's approval. After Ricky had removed his stage makeup and changed into his street clothes, his grandmother came backstage to congratulate him on a job well done. As he sat waiting in his dressing room, Ricky anticipated a pleasant reaction, but he never expected that his depiction of Marius would bring tears to her eyes. This was all the approbation he would need.

After laughing, crying, and reminiscing with his number one fan, his grandmother, Ricky was invited to attend the cast party. Everyone from the cast members to the crew to the show's producers were there to celebrate Ricky's achievement. Seeing that his rehearsal time was unusually brief, they had been apprehensive about Ricky's performance. The show's success gave everyone a reason to rejoice. Ricky's resonant depiction of a young man's quest for truth and justice had touched them deeply, and they spent the whole night patting him on the back. Proud as could be, Ricky readily accepted their compliments, and went to his new home a happy man. "I believe that my theatrical debut in New York could not have been more interesting" he said.

The audiences seemed to concur, swooning whenever Ricky broke into song with the moving ballad "Empty Chairs at Empty Tables" and the passionate duet "A Heart Full of Love." One theater critic for *Newsday* reported that a throng of teenage fans were gathering to get a glimpse of Ricky before each performance. Never before had the Imperial Theater seen anything like Ricky Martin.

Summing up his contribution to the Broadway scene, a reviewer for *Latin Music Online* wrote, "Although not in possession of a classically trained voice, Ricky Martin sings with honesty and earnestness that fits the character of the young, somewhat idealistic Marius well. Some really lovely material is written for groups of three and four singers throughout the show, and he handles this often difficult ensemble work well. I found his best moment of the evening was during 'A Little Fall of Rain' a gentle, poignant moment as his friend and secret admirer Eponine dies slowly in his arms. Belting out a tune is one thing, but being able to sing softly and with meaning is what moves this writer. His solo 'Empty Tables at Empty Chairs' was performed with the right balance of anger and sadness."

Perusing all the laudatory reviews that his performance as Marius had inspired, an immense surge of pride welled up in Ricky's heart. Not only did he not embarrass himself, as many believed that he would, but he won over the grizzled New York critics. Despite the triumph, Ricky's battle for recognition had only just begun. To keep from falling out of favor with the public, he would have to maintain the quality of his per-

A young Ricky with members of Menudo.
(© Ernie Paniccioli/Retna Ltd, USA)

The members of Menudo at a recording session.
(© Ernie Paniccioli/Retna Ltd, USA)

Even at a young age, his charisma shone through.
(© Ernie Paniccioli/Retna Ltd, USA)

Ricky promoting his super hot album VUELVE at a record store. (© Steve Granitz/Retna Ltd.)

A sharp dresser—he always looks fabulous.
(© Youri Lenquette/Retna Pictures/Retna Ltd, USA)

A gracious Ricky accepts an award for his album.
(© Redferns)

Ricky always has a smile for the cameras.
(© Scott Teitler/Retna Ltd, USA)

His concerts are always high energy and
bring the crowd to their feet. (© Redferns)

Ricky hugs a Grammy for Best Latin Pop Performance,
which he won for his album VUELVE.
(© Steve Granitz/Retna Ltd.)

formance every night for a total of three months.

The routine of portraying the same character on a daily basis was offset by the spontaneity of live performance. Originally, Ricky had thought that the daily depiction of Marius would become as tedious as his work on *General Hospital*. But as he soon discovered, the life of a Broadway actor was nothing if not unpredictable and exciting. "In theater, if you miss . . . you miss," he explained during an America Online chat. "On TV you can cut and start the scene again. [But a theatrical production is] always different, every night. The audience has a lot to do with it."

On one occasion, Ricky had a near collision with Craig Schulman, the actor portraying Valjean. After almost skewering him with his stage-prop sword, Ricky was horrified by the close call. Apologizing repeatedly to Schulman, Ricky's feelings of guilt were allayed only when the veteran actor assured him that "everyone has his story on the barricades, and this will be your first."

Performing before a live audience every night never got any easier. The pressure to please the crowds was considerable. He never knew when the audience would respond favorably, and when they would find fault. Still, he loved being able to take thousands of theatergoers on a musical journey through the past, and worked hard to accomplish exactly that. "Every night you have a tough crowd and you have to win them over," he conveyed to *Hitkrant*. "It's very unpredictable and that is just what I wanted. I don't want an audience that is going to love everything I do, no matter what it is."

Although he had expected to work long and hard, Ricky never foresaw the considerable emotional and physical commitment that acting on Broadway required. After lowering the curtain on one performance, he only had time enough to sleep, take a shower and exercise before having to do it all over again. During his first trip to New York, he'd had ample opportunity to roam the city. But on this occasion, he saw very little of New York's many sights. There was just no way to fit in going out on the town into his already crammed schedule. "Doing a show like *Les Miserables*, eight shows a week, it's exhausting. So you need to rest a lot and take singing lessons regularly. I have to be there at 7:30. Because if you show up at 7:33 then you get a memo and you'll get in trouble!"

After laboring with the theater company for over a month, Ricky was a wreck. He was running out of steam, and needed time to recharge. Knowing that he wasn't necessarily weaker or less disciplined than anyone else, he wondered how other Broadway thespians could keep up with the schedule. During his brief stint with *Les Miserables*, he developed a deep veneration for those actors who go out on stage night after night, admiring the nerves of steel that helped them weather the public's critical storms. "The public of New York is very demanding, but also, when they like something, they know how to demonstrate it," he told CNN. "I feel an enormous respect for the actors who manage to make it on Broadway."

This newfound respect for the theater and its players gave Ricky the chance to forge new friendships in New York. Incessantly asking the veterans questions about his performance, Ricky managed to ingratiate himself into the hearts of fellow cast members. Besides admiring his dedication and desire to learn, many of his co-workers were also secretly in awe of his amazing voice and natural acting talent. All in all, Ricky had only good things to say about the people behind *Les Mise*.

"Working with incredible performers. I've learned a lot from them," he told America Online. "And my favorite scene is when Jean Valjean is going through a cathartic moment telling me his life at the end of the second act. I never felt alone working with the actors that have been doing this show for many years. The directors did an outstanding job."

On September 8, 1996, Ricky took the Broadway stage for his final heart-stopping performance. His three-month run at the Imperial Theater had come to an end. As he watched the curtain fall for the last time, he got choked up with emotion. After hugging his cast-mates and bidding them all a fond farewell, he silently slipped out of their lives. Returning to his apartment, Ricky was both happy to get some rest, and sorry to see his hectic Broadway experience go the way of Menudo. "Of course, once you do theater it becomes kind of addictive and you have to do it again," he explained. "It is one of the most beautiful things I've done in my life. Just being able to sing, dance, and act and have the audience with you at the same time!"

Performing in *Les Miserables* had been everything he hoped it would be, and more. During his tenure, he'd learned that connecting with the audience as a stage actor could induce a euphoria more pronounced than anything he'd felt before. He definitely saw himself repeating the experience at some point in the future. "I'd like to do some Shakespeare in the Park," he told *Soap Opera Weekly*. "I would love to do *Sunset Boulevard* with Betty Buckley. I want Broadway to be a part of my life."

In the meanwhile, however, he was completely drained of all motivation. His time on the stage had worn him out, and Ricky took a long-overdue break to savor everything he had missed during this second trip to New York. He used the two short weeks he had left in Manhattan to resume his favorite pastime—watching pedestrians while relaxing in the park. But unlike his last visit, he used this downtime to collect his thoughts and compose new material for his next album. "New York City is a city with a great personality," he informed America Online. "It inspired me a lot to write my music just sitting on a bench in the park and looking at people's faces."

CHAPTER 6

Go! Go! Go! ... On the Road with Ricky

Coasting from one victory to another, Ricky wasted no time going back on tour after *Les Miserables*. While he had been busy displaying his vocal and acting prowess in the role of Marius, sales of *A Medio Vivir* had been skyrocketing. Jumping on the chance to resume his life of travel and adventure, he went against his manager's advice, and his own initial inclination, by refusing to take a break. To fulfill the public's fervid demand for Ricky, the young performer began preparations for an extensive trek through Spain, France, and Belgium.

By now, traveling had become a way of life. After spending three months in one place, Ricky needed to go mobile. Passive soul searching no longer held any allure for the driven up-and-comer. As the days of his post-Broadway break turned into weeks, he grew restless and yearned to get back to the grindstone. When *Salut* magazine asked him for his thoughts on extended vacations, Ricky responded, "I think I'd become crazy. I need to work, I love it so much. Three months is too long. I've just stopped for a whole month, and if, in the end, they had told me that I could have taken one more week off, I think I'd have begun to panic!"

Instead of resting on his laurels, Ricky was set on expanding his realm of influence. He was about to go global.

Taking his act to an international level, however, required much forethought and preparation. To finalize his agenda of becoming a worldwide superstar, he sought the counsel of one of his biggest role models. "Julio Iglesias, my hero in terms of international career, told me his secret: 'To have success in a country, you need to be there,' " Ricky recalled during a *Star Club* interview. "But I don't want to stop there. I want to be able to come back in fifteen years and still be applauded."

How many people could honestly claim to have stayed in expensive hotels, met new and exciting people from every corner of the globe, and been paid for the privilege. The chance to see the world in its vast entirety was not one Ricky would, or could, take for granted. "Traveling is my dream since I was a little boy," he explained to *Salut*. "Since I have success almost everywhere now, I'm invited throughout the whole world. I make my ideal life a reality. It's great to get to see that many countries. It lets me find nice little places for my next vacations."

Even though the mere mention of Ricky Martin was enough to sell concert tickets, the demand for a tour was enhanced by the continued ubiquity of the hit single "Maria." The song was so popular in Europe that it opened many doors that had, heretofore, remained firmly closed. Number one in France, Australia, Belgium, and Spain, "Maria" became the second top-selling single of 1997. Years after it had been released, Ricky's name would still be associated with the song's infectious rhythms and beat. "It's great. It's like the song has its own life and I'm not going to interfere," he relayed to *Cleo*. " 'Maria' was picked up first in Latin America and then, in France, it became the biggest-selling single last year."

While "Maria" was responsible for thrusting Ricky past the guardians of European music lines, its success threatened to overshadow his artistry and subsequent recording efforts. Because Ricky the performer had become inextricably linked with the single, Ricky the artist stood in danger of being overlooked. Concerned about his professional longevity, he worried that the international community would confuse him with just another flash in the pan.

"From South America to Spain is just a small step," he leveled with *Hitkrant*. "And the album, and especially the single 'Maria,' is having a lot of success in France, Belgium, Germany, Finland . . . it's great! But what I find more important than just dropping by now is that in ten years time I can come back and still get the Dutch people dancing or get them into a romantic mood with my music. I don't want to be just another summer hype. I know I'm not very popular here yet and I know I have to work hard, but I don't mind that. I also know that there are always artists appearing who have one big hit and you'll never see them again, but I don't want to be like that. I don't want to be dramatic, but this is my career, my life, my all!"

Spain was the first stop on Ricky's jam-packed itinerary. Due to the lack of a language barrier, Ricky felt comfortable launching his European conquest on Spanish soil. Before the dawning of "Maria," Spain had been somewhat resistant to Latin music. A vital part of Europe, the country championed the same U.S. and Euro-pop rhythms as the rest of the Continent.

But Ricky changed all that.

His arrival lured hundreds of fans to his airport terminal and thousands more to his concerts. While other artists had unsuccessfully tried to make a run for the Spanish border, it was Ricky's humble attitude toward his music and his international fans that clinched his victory over the nation. "It's focusing, it's giving a lot of respect to the audience and being there," Ricky explained to the *Union-Tribune*. "Going straight to the country and promoting and saying, 'Hi, nice to meet you.' "

Having won over the Spanish market, Ricky turned his compass needle to the east, and set his sights on France. If he thought Spain was a difficult country to penetrate, he was in for a rude awakening. Better-known artists, like Gloria Estefan, had tried and failed to elicit a hearty handshake from the country that coined the term "elite." Ricky worried that the finicky French consumers would meet him with an equally lackluster reception.

His fears, as it turned out, were completely unfounded. Masses of fans came out to see Ricky's high-octane performances. One of the most popular guests on French television shows and a permanent fixture in French magazines, his arrival was one of the most talked about events of the year. Not since Julio Iglesias had a Latin performer received such a magnanimous welcome. "My success in France made me a lot more mature! In your country, I've learned individuality and to believe in my convictions," he told *Star Club*. "The French market is extremely hard to be popular in. That's why I consider this achievement like a victory against myself and against a market that was before completely closed to Latino music."

Having visited France on one prior occasion, Ricky knew a thing or two about the country's rich cultural heritage and vibrant landscape. During his first trip, he'd had the pleasure of visiting Paris's renowned museums, taking in the unparalleled sights and walking along the Seine. The experience was so memorable, that the singer never failed to set aside some time to stop at a few of the city's famous landmarks, nightclubs, and theaters. But of all the attractions held out by the City of Light, his favorite remained the promenades along the river.

"When I'm in Paris and I have time off, if you are looking for me, you'll always find me on the quay [river bank]," he revealed to *Salut*. "I love the Seine! That river makes me feel so romantic. I like to stroll in the wind, just for the fun of it, and if I find myself near a museum, I run inside. I have this passion for art. Last time, I visited the Orsay Museum and the Louvre, where I got to see Leonardo DaVinci's Mona Lisa. What a feeling!"

Part of what made Ricky such a phenomenon in France, Spain, and around the world was his charismatic and powerful stage presence. Known for his elaborate showcases, complete with lights, sounds, vibrant musicians, and dancers, Ricky's much-talked about concerts captivated audiences young and old. A natural on stage, he prides himself on being a showman first and a singer second. "I've been performing on stage since I was six years old—and I still haven't found a word that can describe these feelings," he asserted to *HiT!* "To name a few: power, self-assurance, adrenaline, strength . . . It's addictive and it's fascinating. One hour on stage makes up for years of hard work."

Addicted to the endorphin high that his live presentations brought about, Ricky thrived on performing for his screaming fans. So much so that the mere idea of taking a break from touring scared him. Dependent upon the mass affirmation of his nightly cheering section, he would tour for long stretches of time, without ever stopping to rest. "When you're on stage, all your senses are very vulnerable," he conveyed to CNN. "The band is playing behind you. You see people singing to your music, dancing to your rhythms. You try it once, you don't want to let go."

No two concerts were ever the same. Ricky put every ounce of his strength and energy into each and every show. Providing the biggest bang for the ticket holder's buck was his top priority. Yet even though he has fond memories of every live performance, one concert experience stands out brightly from the rest. "I did a marvelous show in Buenos Aires, Argentina, I'll tell you the story quickly," he told *Bravo*. "It was the biggest stage, the biggest show I had prepared, there were going to be 250,000 people. They were giving me a diamond record [more than a million and a half copies], all the press was going to be there . . . and suddenly, because of politics, they wanted to cancel it five days before. Finally the show went on, it was a success, and I ended up crying in my room!"

Many of Ricky's fans wonder what goes into planning a show of such mythic proportions. Contrary to popular belief, smoke, mirrors, and technical wizardry are not nearly as important as good, old-fashioned hard work. Before he ever takes the stage, Ricky has already devoted many months to practice and rehearsal. Making sure that everyone knows their role and can carry out their responsibilities, he is involved in every aspect of the painstaking tour preparation process. "I am the one who takes control of it all . . . of course there are the dancers, musicians, and all, but I am the one facing the audience," he informed *La Entrevista*. "I have been working for seven months putting it together because I wanted to make it big. I think Ricky Martin has grown within the last few years.''

Not only do Ricky's concerts speak volumes about his vitality as a performer, they also reveal a lot about his multicultural awareness. As an international sensation, he lives to celebrate people of all backgrounds and ethnicities. This commitment to diversity extends well beyond his willingness to travel to foreign lands; Ricky also incorporates a cornucopia of influences into his own stage show. "I'm totally for melting and mixing cultures," he asserted to *Star Club*. "When you mix two elements, nature keeps only the best ingredients. On stage, for example, I've hired musicians and dancers from around the world! We are eleven on stage, from Puerto Rico, Cuba, Israel, Poland, Mexico, Bulgaria. People from all around the world for music of the world!''

Even with all of this strategic planning and organization, Ricky still manages to retain an element of impulsiveness in his concerts. To him, spontaneity can mean the difference between an event that is stupendous and one that is stupor-inducing. To create a sense of excitement, he must sublimate some of his controlling tendencies in favor of a more organic approach. While the lights, sound, and fireworks displays have to run like clockwork, Ricky refuses to preplan his own fancy footwork. "My movements are not choreographed. It is what comes from my heart," he assured *El Nueve Herald*. "I had choreographed dances in Menudo for years. I don't want any more choreographies.''

And choreography isn't the only thing that Ricky leaves to chance. While his looks may be the stuff of glossy magazine covers, Ricky believes that the less time spent worrying about his physical appearance, the better. Thanks to mother nature's inordinate generosity, he can preselect his wardrobe and rest assured that the stylists will take care of the rest. In the meantime, he busies himself by trying to achieve peace of mind. "The thing that really interests me is the inside of a person," he informed *Bravo*. "Since I was young, the only thing I've really fought for is to develop my inner self. Looking for tranquility, understanding . . . It gives me a lot of strength . . . a day doesn't go by when I don't meditate."

Through meditation, he has been able to keep his ego in check and his priorities in line. While it is Ricky who pulls out all the stops for each and every concert, he's under no illusion that the evening is all about him. He sees his fans as the real stars, and tries to pamper them accordingly. "If I stay backstage for too long with nothing to do, it makes me crazy! I want to bring them comfort," he said referring to his audiences. "When I go on stage, I tell myself I'm there to make people forget all their worries and to have a blast with them! And even if some of my songs are about the sad realities of this world, I want to make them understand the message in a nonaggressive way."

Even though he often wonders whether his fans are enjoying their concert experience, Ricky can rest assured that everyone is having a good time. Judging by the many flowers and risqué souvenirs flying through the air at any given moment, it's safe to assume that the audience has no cause for complaint. Just to be sure, however, Ricky had a tendency to frequently address his loyal devotees during each show. "I plan very dynamic concerts," he confirmed to *Bravo*. "The stage will be an authentic 'fiesta' . . . The shows will last about an hour and a half, more or less, depending on how much I talk, because you know that when I start talking, no one can stop me!''

Conversations are all well and good, but when things heat up, the communication between onlookers and performer can take a turn for the nonverbal. Instances of fans showing their appreciation by taking off their clothes are too numerous to mention. Although outer garments are the first to go, there are those uninhibited souls, possibly the worse for substances, who insist on showing the full monty. ''During summertime, some people take off their shirts, their pants, while dancing,'' he revealed to *Salut*. ''It doesn't happen really often, but I've seen people taking it all off! I think it's cute in a way.''

An orgiastic blur of wine, women, and song, Ricky's concerts see the performer functioning on all eight cylinders. Standing at the head of the Dionysian jubilee and offering up his lyrical toast to the god of revelry, it is clear to one and all that he is truly at home.

Of course, all good things must come to an end. When the fervor and elation of the live show subside, Ricky tends to get somewhat melancholy. After seeing so many fans screaming his name and singing along with his songs, it's hard for him to relax and unwind in his lonely hotel room. ''I take a cold bath and I eat,'' he reported matter-of-factly to *Salut*. ''Then, I try to stay active because after two hours of labor in front of a crowd that's constantly applauding you, you feel a bit high! And if I can't keep my feet on the ground, I'd become crazy! Since I don't want to go to sleep with all that tension inside of me, I call friends and talk to them about the concert!''

While Ricky could never be faulted for trying to skate by on looks alone, there is no denying that his impossibly pretty face and body have helped his career tremendously. Yet the outward attributes offer only a hint of what's to come. If Ricky had not had the talent and charisma to back up his promising appearance, his life in show business would have ended as surely as his career with Menudo.

As things stand, the entertainer is the complete package and the real deal. Possessing a deadly combination of looks, vocals, and easy confidence, he is simply irresistible to women of all ages and nationalities. Just one glance at the fiery performer swiveling his infamous hips onstage is enough to send millions of girls into fits of hysteria. A sex symbol since the age of twelve, Ricky never gets used to the pandemonium. Far from exulting in the effect which he has on women, Ricky often complains of the horrifying chaos his presence creates.

"There are moments when I fear a little," he admitted during an interview. "Actually, I hate security forces and bodyguards, but, sometimes, they are necessary. Once, I left a concert in an ambulance [to avoid crowds] but a girl approached the car and broke the windscreen with a bottle. I also can't forget a girl who threw a bottle at my head shouting: 'Ricky, I love you!' Surely, if she wanted to be remembered, she succeeded in it."

On one occasion some obsessed fans went too far, sneaking into his room while he was trying to sleep after a big concert. While the stunt may have seemed like a funny way to meet their dream man to the girls who'd pulled it, Ricky was not amused. "Once, in New York, I was lying on my bed, and I heard little weird noises," he recounted the scary incident to *Salut*. "I got up and looked everywhere. Under the bed: nothing! Behind the door: nothing! In the bathroom: still noth-

ing! You'll never guess where they were; they were
hiding in the aeration pipe! They had been more clever
than all the private eyes put together!"

Although this enthusiastic fanbase has done wonders
for Ricky's career, it does nothing to aid his quest for
privacy and solitude. Since his rise to international stardom, he has had to become adept at blending into the
background. A master of disguise, he takes pleasure in
outsmarting some of his more ardent admirers and
overprotective security guards. "Sometimes I sneak
past the security and leave my hotel," he confided in
Hitkrant. "I go in disguise with a hat on, or something
like that, and I go walking or cycling. If I don't have
my bike with me, I rent one. My security guards never
agree with this, but suddenly they'll see me going past.
Then I'll give them a friendly wave, as if to say, 'I did
it again! Ha ha ha!' "

Yet its not only Ricky's fans and guards who keep
him from enjoying time on his own. Everyone from his
manager to his roadies to his publicist to the members
of his touring company are to blame for the star's
escape-artist tactics. As long as he's surrounded by his
entourage, he can't forget that he is a superstar. Sometimes running away from it all for an hour or two is
all Ricky needs to remember how lucky he really is.

"I require long hours of silence," he informed the
Philippine Daily Inquirer. "I make sure my mind is
clear from any negative things and my body is well
rested. After that, it's all about feelings and emotions
and passion. You need to always go back to your be-
ginnings, recharge your batteries and keep your feet
where they are suppose to be—on the ground. I'm constantly moving from one place to another, and sometimes I have to be reminded where I am going to or
coming from, so I will know how to proceed."

*   *.   *

The life of a wanderer has always appealed to Ricky, but only to a point. After a while, he begins to feel displaced from his familiar environment and years for a sense of constancy. While owning private homes in Puerto Rico, Miami, Los Angeles, and Buenos Aires may seem like a luxury to most, for Ricky it is a matter of basic survival. "What happens is that I travel a lot and I get tired of the hotel life, I try to feel like home, so I can really rest; at each house I have my own clothes and my stuff," he explained. "Thus, when I travel to these places I don't need to worry about packing."

No matter how hard he tries to eschew the impersonal hotel rooms, these have become his lot in life. The nearly identical, albeit extravagant, accommodations that he encounters on his tours can leave him feeling as if he's all alone in the world. Never without a picture of his family, Ricky looks to these images of domestic bliss and comfort to combat feelings of homesickness. "I always take photos of my grandmother, the most beautiful person on earth. And of my mother. They're very important to me and they give me support and strength when I need it."

Part of what made the young man rely so heavily on his family's support was his need to resist the illusions of grandeur constantly reinforced by touring. Firmly ensconced within a huge framework of enraptured co-workers and fans, Ricky needed to call upon every possible resource to keep egomania at bay. The road—with all its temptation to buy into his own publicity and begin referring to all noncelebrities as "the little people"—was a far cry from the stabling influence his home in Puerto Rico provided.

"The enemy of my life is the word 'fame,' " Ricky stated to *Diversion*. "This is somewhat ironic because an artist is constantly looking for the acceptance of the public and the applause of the people telling you how good you are. This can disorient you at any moment and it can leave you in pieces. I insist there is nothing nicer than applause, because it is the food and the motivation, but not if you do not know how to fight it and how to handle it. I just have to remember how we have seen the legend made and I do not want to be one more of those who fall into drugs or other artificial things. I am not into that; I look for a silent moment every day, to meditate, to do well, to listen, to speak to myself, to make logical decisions."

Living on the run also makes it virtually impossible for Ricky to benefit from the joys of a secure and loving relationship. The demands of his career are such that he is never in one place for too long. Unfortunately, most women cannot tolerate such lengthy separations. Thus, at least for now, his career must take precedence. Still, Ricky looks forward to a day when he can stop touring and start a family. "I think that to travel constantly makes this complicated, because a woman always looks for a more stable life. It's difficult, because at the moment my priority is my career."

Despite his perpetual battle to squelch his need for love, Ricky's romantic side does get the better of him on occasion. After being on the road for what seemed an eternity, he pledged to find the woman of his dreams, regardless of the sacrifice it entailed. "Today, my goal is to have a family, a wife," he admitted to *Salut*. "I know it's hard with the kind of work I do. But I refuse to believe it's impossible! When Cupid will come and make a hole in my heart with his arrow,

I will fall in love no matter if I'm famous or not, no matter if I'm a singer or not. I will fall in love like everybody else.''

During his frequent voyages throughout the world, Ricky was like a thirsty man afloat in a pool of fresh water. Unable to make a move without some attractive woman throwing herself at his feet, he tried to exercise self-control by separating fantasy from reality. With so much enticement around him, many have wondered whether Ricky could indeed tame his primal urges. Three years and zero paternity suits later, he seems to have succeeded in subduing, if not gelding, the stallion within.

Ricky's conservative take on casual sex is rooted mostly in his search for true love. He's determined to find someone who is interested in him for more than his resume of smoldering good looks, worldwide fame, and substantial wealth. ''There's still authenticity, you know,'' he told the *Los Angeles Times*. ''It's hard to find it, but it exists. There's a whole world out there of people who don't watch TV, don't listen to the radio, people who are not into music. You encounter girls like that, and it feels good.''

Biding his time until he fell in love, Ricky poured all of his passion into his work. While there were many downsides to living out of a suitcase, there were just as many benefits that kept Ricky's spirits high throughout his European trek. His obsession with meeting and learning from locals was a testament to his empathetic and tolerant nature. While many celebrities site money and promotional opportunities as their main reasons for extensive travel, Ricky legitimately enjoyed immersing himself in different cultures. As he explained to *CBS This Morning*, ''When you travel so much, you meet so many people in different countries. It's just fascinating to be able to interact with other people, with other ways of thinking.''

During one trip to Buenos Aries, Ricky escaped from the throngs of fans waiting outside his hotel to attend an informal concert. It was there that he finally found the local flavor he'd been looking for. ''I put myself through a bedspread inside a travel bag to get rid of the press and the fans and I said to the driver: 'Take me to the most Argentine quarter of Buenos Aires where we can find the true Tango,' '' he recounted during an interview with *Aló* magazine. ''We were five friends, two Argentines and three Puerto Ricans. We found ourselves singing and dancing Tango with the owner of the guitar and an old man who was eighty years old with a beard and a sombrero. And this was the most exciting concert we did. It was bohemia. That's what I'm going to do constantly. When I go to Andalucía, I'll hear the true Flamenco.''

At the peak of his romp through Europe, Ricky came face to face with his greatest enemy—exhaustion.

Never one to complain, the performer vowed to ride out the grueling schedule. But the constant exertion was beginning to take a toll on his health. After bringing the tour to a premature close, even Ricky had to admit that he had come dangerously close to a total collapse. ''I've worked a lot last year, but I don't blame anybody, not even myself,'' he told *Salut*. ''We were all very excited to work that much, we've had a lot of fun, and that's what's important. I think that if I did even more, it could have been a catastrophe, but I've stopped at the right moment.''

When news of the cancelled concert dates broke, everyone speculated about the cause. Those who had not yet had a chance to see Ricky in person were stumped for an explanation. What could have happened to the strapping young man? Did he have a nervous breakdown, as some had contended? It was up to Ricky to put an end to the gossip. "I didn't collapse or anything," he explained, "but I had done a couple of countries in one day again, and I was just tired out."

What seemed like an unlucky break at the time, turned out to be one of the best things that could have happened to Ricky. Time off was just what he needed to recover his senses and recuperate from his exhaustion. Even though he was forced to relax by the doctors, he discovered that taking care of his health was something he owed to himself. Spending his free time in a beautiful Miami mansion, Ricky reacquainted himself with the art of staying still.

"I stayed in my new house in Miami. I relaxed, did a lot of sports, ate healthy, and saw my family," he told *Salut*. "I also had a lot of moments by myself, which I missed last year. I read a lot, decorated my bedroom with paintings of South American artists, I did 'normal' things. Seeing my family helped me recharge my batteries to the maximum."

Ricky was so content with his new lifestyle that he vowed to reevaluate his future touring engagements. He would never again compromise his well-being. While his fans were still at the top of his priority roster, he realized that a sick and tired Ricky Martin is of no use to anyone. "I know how far I can push myself," he asserted. "I told the record company that after every fifteen days I want a couple of days off. Look, visiting four countries in three days is something I'll keep doing because I love doing it. But it mustn't go on for too long. From now on I'll do it for fifteen days in a row, and then I may have five days off."

Emerging from one of his most demanding tours to

date, Ricky had learned a lot about his limitations, his abilities, and his potential. Having blown the lid off Europe's once impenetrable domain, he was finally confident in his own success. Most important, he now knew how to reconcile his professional and personal obligations. Ready to explore and conquer new terrain, Ricky looked forward to his next journey.

CHAPTER 7

A Herculean Feat

The year 1997 was replete with sudden discoveries, travel to exotic locales, and revolutionary ideas. Besides using his music to pierce through the heart of the European community, Ricky also had the pleasure of starring in Disney's animated feature film *Hercules*. While actor Tate Donovan had played the lead in the English version, Ricky was asked to reprise the role of the mythical hero for the film's Spanish version in May of 1997.

When the Disney executives called with the request, the young performer was taken off guard. He had no idea that he was even being considered for the role. But while he had been busy rounding off his tour of Europe, the film's producers were evaluating him behind closed doors. "The reason they trust me is because they did their homework," Ricky told *Latin Style*. "They went through everything I'd done. They talked to a lot of people that I've worked with. I'm talking about different producers, different directors, et cetera, so they could trust me."

When asked to play the leading role, Ricky marveled at his good fortune. Disney was known for casting only the most talented of actors and vocalists. Realizing that the offer was a considerable honor, he was quick to accept the role. Also, as part of his contribution, Ricky recorded an original song titled "No Importanta La Distancia" and an accompanying video.

Working on *Hercules* was more challenging than he could have ever anticipated. The pressure to deliver a top-of-the-line performance for the benefit of the Hispanic market was considerable. But, as always, Ricky rose to the occasion admirably. By committing himself to practicing his lines and delivery on a daily basis, he was able to make the role of Hercules come alive.

"Well, it's a big responsibility. It's like opening doors to a different culture, to where I come from, to my people. If I do it right, they will trust us and they will keep counting on us. I got in touch with the character. I worked a lot on it. I studied it. I watched the movie a couple of times. I went into the beauty of Greek mythology, and I became part of the film. It's fascinating. It's something I had never done before, so of course, I gave one hundred percent."

Locked in a sound booth for hours on end, Ricky used his imagination to bring his character to life. If Hercules was fighting in a battle, Ricky would have to imagine how it would feel to don a protective shield and wield a sword. If he was performing a love scene, Ricky would have to pretend that his leading lady was beside him. He would also have to find a different voice that would more accurately depict the animated Hercules. Luckily, his vocal training simplified this process considerably. While some of the most renowned actors have to seek help from speech coaches, Ricky was able to pronounce his words with perfect intonation and pitch.

In an interview with *Latin Style*, he compared the *Les Miserables* experience with that of making *Her-*

cules: "*Les Miserables* was physically exhausting while *Hercules* was mentally exhausting. When I say mentally exhausting, I mean I have to use the acting techniques that I usually use to help me animate something. It's completely different. It's simply fascinating! It's something that I want to do . . . that I would love to do again."

While making the movie gave Ricky the chance to work with one of the world's largest film studios, it was his love for children that really attracted him to the project. One of his personal missions in life is helping and providing for children with AIDS. Touched by their stories and plights, Ricky makes a concerted effort to reach out to kids he now considers part of his own extended family. "I am the sponsor of a Puerto Rican hospital for children with AIDS, and I also support a school for disabled babies, which carries my name," he expressed to *TV Guide*. "This is something very special, mainly when I can spend the time to be with them. We never lose contact, because wherever I am, I send them a video in which I tell them how much I miss them."

Although Ricky is proud of his contribution, he never loses sight of the real heroes. In fact, he believes that it's the children who are actually doing *him* a favor. After spending many hours with the kids, he quickly realized how much they had to offer. "There are twenty-two AIDS-infected kids who are like my god children in Puerto Rico," he told *Salut*. "They know they're going to die, but they still smile. That's a real lesson of life."

Acting as the voice of Hercules gave Ricky the chance to give something back to the children of the world. The chance to brighten the lives of young people was extremely rewarding. And even though Ricky had come face to face with some of the world's toughest critics, he was even more nervous about the feedback he would get from his younger audience. "I am dealing with kids and that is the toughest audience there could ever be," he confirmed to *Latin Style*. "Because of society, adults are more diplomatic, kids are pure. If they don't like it, they'll say it. They'll get bored, stand up, and leave. It doesn't matter if they are in a movie theater. In that case, my motto was to keep them with me at all times through my voice."

To Ricky's surprise and utter relief, his performance in *Hercules* met with a positive reaction from all camps. Children turned out to see the film in droves, and adults were just as captivated by the animated images and songs as their offspring. The single "No Importanta La Distancia" even soared to the top of the Latin charts. Much like his animated persona, Hercules, Ricky proved that nothing was beyond his reach.

Since 1996, Ricky had been working steadily on his fourth album. But it wasn't until December 1997 that Ricky relocated to Miami in order to complete the much-anticipated project. Located just a few miles from the studio, Ricky moved into a stately new home situated in an exclusive community that is home to celebrities such as Madonna and Gloria Estefan. Since touring had been keeping him from finishing the new album, the move was critical to his career. More important, however, was the effect it had on his state of mind.

Although the demand for Ricky had not let up, and his days were still a dizzying round of promotional events and concert appearances, he finally had a place to call home. "The house that I rent in Miami is just sublime," he told *Star Club*. "It has a gigantic swimming pool in which I love to swim. But to be exact, I haven't rented it to spend a vacation. It's clearly a workplace where I go between two TV shows or two concerts. Some days, I don't even get to see the daylight because I'm in my studio. I'm an unremitting worker. My music always comes first. I love what I do so much!''

A chance to finish his latest album in peace and quiet was not the only thing Florida had to offer. Miami offered Ricky plenty of opportunities to spend time with his family and friends, whom he had missed while canvassing the globe. With one half-brother residing right in the city and another one close enough to visit, Ricky was at last able to catch up on some overdue bonding. His mother also rested easier knowing that Ricky had someone to look out for him. ''In Florida, I'm closer to Puerto Rico and then my brothers can visit me more times,'' he told *Bravo*. ''My half-brother Eric lives in Miami, too, where he studies aeronautic mechanics at a university. On holidays, my other brother, Daniel, visits me for a month. He is thirteen years old and he is super-active. He is always moving. I asked my friends if they wanted to help me entertain him because I didn't have enough energy for that much activity.''

While Ricky spent most of his time in the studio, his life was by no means all work and no play. When time allowed, he made the most of it by throwing elaborate poolside soirées. With a menu concocted by some of Miami's greatest caterers, bright lights illuminating the pool, and music courtesy of his favorite Latin artists, Ricky's parties were some of the most wild and exclusive in Miami. Everyone wanted to receive an invitation, if only for the chance to hear Ricky belt out a tune, but only a few were granted that special privilege.

While they were truly memorable, the parties grew few and far between as Ricky committed himself to wrapping up the fourth album. In the meanwhile, he shared his house with his faithful pooch Icaro and his personal maid Maria. "My housekeeper, Maria, she moved to Miami with the family too," he informed *Bravo*. "She came to San Salvador, is married to a Puerto Rican, and she lives very close to me. She treats me like a son, she cooks typical dishes of Puerto Rico and watches Icaro when I'm traveling."

Besides Maria, he received very few visitors. Ricky preferred to be left alone to write in his journal, read, surf, or rock climb. But whenever the mood to cut loose and have some fun would strike, he would indulge in his latest obsession—the race track. "I go racing. Whenever I can spare the time you can find me on the race course," said Ricky. "Nothing in the world gives me a greater kick than racing. If I hadn't become an artist, I would have become a race car driver. You can be sure of that!"

Alas, the young star's Indy 500 dreams would not be realized. Racing to complete his album would be the closest he would get to life in the fast lane. The fully equipped recording studio would be his second home for the next few months. Yet, Ricky didn't mind staying inside the trenches. The fourth album had been plaguing him ever since he had started it two years prior. As he explained to *Salut*, "I started recording it in 1996! It's crazy, when you think of it: it almost took me two years! Every time I had a couple of days off, I went to the studio in Miami to record."

Trying to exceed the high-water mark set by his previous effort, *A Medio Vivir*, Ricky decided to make *Vuelve* his most socially conscious album to date. His tours throughout the world had opened his eyes to a variety of social issues and problems. The idea that poverty, disease, war, and even famine existed at a time when he was content and satisfied didn't sit well with Ricky. Always willing to lend a helping hand to those in need, he recognized music's power to bring about positive changes in the world and vowed to create a record that would make people stop and think. "When I look back, I sometimes tell myself that my music is too 'pop and love,' " he admitted to *Star Club*. "More and more, I want to explore social matters in my songs. It will actually be the tone of my next Spanish album, that I just finished recording."

Reflecting upon his past voyages, Ricky could not deny that there were many things to be celebrated as well. With every injustice or problem he spotted, there was always a life-affirming image like a magnificent sunset, a haunting melody, or a beautiful woman to counteract his melancholy. Ricky, therefore, decided that his next album would paint a comprehensive picture of life, complete with all its sorrows and all its joys.

"The truth of the matter is that I began to comprehend that rhythms entered the world when it was time to sing about your happiness and your sadness," he expressed to *El Nuevo Día*. "This album has a little of everything. We sing of love, life, women, and hope from a serious and existential point of view. People will be able to enjoy all sides of this piece of work."

A geographical and emotional travelogue of sorts, *Vuelve* documented Ricky's experiences while on tour. Some of the most energetic and upbeat tracks were generated by the intrinsic pleasure Ricky derived from these excursions. "It was inspired by all my vacations, and I think we feel a particular energy when we listen to it," he informed *Salut*. "On this album, all my influences are mixed together. Result: it's joyful, it makes you want to dance, at least, I think.''

Global in content and style, *Vuelve* drew inspiration from the music of each country. Since Ricky had been melding different cultures on stage for the past year, it seemed only natural to re-create some of that magic in the studio. ''I spent six weeks in Brazil just looking for music,'' he expressed to *Estylo*. ''I went to the *Carnival* in Brazil. Brazil had a lot of influence on the actual music of *Vuelve*. We have to mix all these sounds. We have to do anything to keep music alive. I am just presenting myself as who I am, fusion.''

The creation of *Vuelve* was Ricky's effort to unite the world by one common cause of celebration and mutual understanding. But even as he tried to reach out to throngs of people around the world, Ricky didn't want to lose sight of who he was or where he came from. The album, therefore, struck a unique chord in that it was, at once, entirely personal and profoundly universal. ''I think I have evolved over the years,'' he told *Radiff on the Net*. ''In this album, I've used some of the unique sounds that I've picked up from different continents. The sounds, the rhythms are very earthy. But I will not change the base—it is very Puerto Rican. I don't want to change that, not even for the next album I am working on.''

While Puerto Rico still held a primary place in Ricky's heart, he wanted *Vuelve* to be accessible to people from different backgrounds. For two years, he had researched different musical styles, working with national artists and listening carefully to what he heard. Thanks to this painstaking process, he knew exactly what the new album should sound like.

Now it was time to look inward.

Although a time limit couldn't be set on this critical

task, Ricky was forced to speed up the internal investigation. To facilitate the dive into the inner depths of his soul, Ricky decided to record his thoughts in a journal; ideas that he could pull from when it came time to compose new songs. At that point in his life, being honest with himself and his fans was of vital importance. "I do not want to wear a mask, I want my album to reflect who I am," he told *Salut*. "I am working with the same team as my last album, and I am very glad of the work done until now, and we will put all our energy toward succeeding in this new project."

The fruitful collaboration that began on *A Medio Vivir* would continue on *Vuleve*. The reasons Ricky elected to regroup with K.C. Porter and Robi Rosa were twofold. First, they were extremely proficient in the production capacity, and, second, they knew Ricky inside and out. It was a match made in recording heaven. Porter and Rosa understood his likes, dislikes, and goals. In fact, while making Ricky's last album, the team had grown so close that they could actually finish each other's sentences.

The record company had set a firm deadline. There was no more room for procrastination. Ricky needed people who would understand his vision without his having to explain it twice. Porter and Rosa *were* these people; they understood him instinctively. So in the interest of time and quality, the two were brought in to oversee the production of *Vuelve*. "You can't afford to be mediocre·in this business," Ricky told the *Los Angeles Times*. "Latin pop has become plastic, like bubble gum. I'm not judging anybody. I'm only talking about me. I'm not a conformist, and I surround myself with people that are like me."

By now, Ricky, Porter, and Rosa were old friends. When Ricky came to them and explained what he wanted the album to achieve, they heard him loud and clear. Bracing themselves for what promised to be a monumental undertaking, the group set about crafting Ricky Martin's most commercially and artistically successful album to date. "When you start a project you have to be positive but you also have to be aggressive," Ricky elaborated to *South China Morning Post*. "If you desire a little house, you will get a little house. But if you want a big house, sooner or later you will get one. The people I work with start with no negative thoughts. We start thinking big, but with our feet on the ground. We know we have to battle and fight for what we want. We decided to take it one step at a time."

Ricky's commitment to artistic development and experimentation was made evident by everything from his choice of producers and composers to the long hours he spent working at the studio. Despite the time constraints, he was adamant about perfecting each track, and never compromised his vision or the album's integrity. And even though the task at hand virtually ruled out any thoughts of a personal life, it was precisely this demanding approach to making music that earned Ricky the respect of his colleagues. "Ricky is somebody who has taken the required steps into true artistry by tapping into his innermost essence, both musically and philosophically," K.C. Porter reported to the *Los Angeles Times*. "He is a perfectionist, but at the same time a very trusting man, which is wonderful for a producer. There's no better relationship you can have with an artist."

The great rapport shared by Ricky and his crew was a great boon for the work-in-progress. There were no rules in the studio, and everyone could voice their opinions freely. A liberated and carefree atmosphere allowed each participant to explore and improvise with new sounds, instruments, and musical motifs. As Ricky explained to *El Nuevo Dia*, his yen for the new and the different stemmed from his own eclectic musical background, as well as that of his collaborators. "Robi and I are from the Caribbean, and, together, since we were young, we have lived the experience of being in Spain and Latin America. This combination motivates us to experiment with a fusion and add a special seal to our music."

During the process of choosing and organizing *Vuelve*'s tracks, Ricky received a call that forced him to reevaluate his game plan. He could hardly believe his ears. On the other end of the receiver was none other than former French soccer star, Michel Platini. Ricky was being asked to participate in World Cup, France, 1998.

With billions of viewers tuning into the broadcast, the World Cup would provide Ricky with his greatest audience yet. In the U.S., the largest sporting event known to man is the Super Bowl; for the rest of the planet, it is undoubtedly the World Cup. What is known as football in the States is called "American football" in every other nation. For the world at large, soccer is the true football, and the World Cup the true Super Bowl. Teams from every country duke it out all season long, each fighting for the right to play in the World Cup, the most widely watched sporting event in the galaxy.

That year, Michel Platini was in charge of organizing the World Cup extravaganza. A fan of Ricky's internationally flavored sound, he thought that "Maria" would make for a great theme song. Not only would Ricky have to give permission to use the song, but he would also be asked to perform the number during the opening ceremony. While Ricky was honored, and wanted nothing so much as to comply, he had to tell Platini that "Maria" was out of commission. Having sung this tune on a thousand different occasions, he felt that it wouldn't be right to rehash the same old song for the biggest event of the year.

Fortunately, the conversation didn't end there.

"When Michel Platini called me to use 'Maria' for the World Cup '98, I told him no," Ricky explained to *Teenager*. "I wanted to do something similar, but another song!"

Giving over complete creative control to Ricky, Platini's only stipulation was that he create a hit on a par with "Maria." Of course, that was easier said than done. Without a doubt, Ricky was versed in the ways of writing songs filled with unforgettable hooks and irresistible rhythms, but to guarantee a hit? Could he really do it? The pressure was considerable, but Ricky was thrilled with the opportunity. "It was very exciting and really important to me," he told *Star Club*. "It was an occasion to melt poetry, music, sports, politics and great passions all together. I had sung at the Olympics with Julio Iglesias and Gloria Estefan. But this time, it was different."

In Ricky's estimation, the World Cup eclipsed the Olympics in both importance and personal meaning. Soccer had always been his favorite sport, he attended matches whenever he had the chance and never missed a World Cup championship. To communicate the thrill of the sport with his song became an all-consuming passion. "I have been working on this project for nearly six months now recording the song, getting closer and closer to the actual sport—it's been a fascinating journey," he said. "The song is full of dreams—I am a football fan—and what I feel when

I'm in the stadium is what I wanted to present through the music.''

A formidable challenge, producing another hit like ''Maria'' required extensive work and hard time in the studio. Ricky also decided that it would be better to bring in a producer with a fresh perspective, someone who had not had a hand in the making *Vuelve*. Titled ''La Copa de la Vida'' (The Cup of Life), the song was handed over to one of the music industry's top producers, Desmond Child, whose credits included arranging albums for such heavyweights as Bon Jovi, Aerosmith, Kiss, and many others.

Maintaining the fusion of styles found on *Vuelve*, ''La Copa de la Vida'' was a rousing and danceable number. Ricky was so proud of the final result, he knew that the World Cup organization would feel the same way. ''When I made that song I did it with lots of energy, good energy,'' he reported to *Teenager*. ''I made it with great composers and producers. It's a song that not only has South American rhythms, but from all parts of the world, like African and Asian. Honestly and humbly, it had everything to be a success. The lyrics are very accessible to people of different languages: Olé, olé, allez. Allez, go, go! . . . It's very easy!''

His opinion about the song's merits were right on target. Only one week would go by before it was eagerly accepted as the official World Cup theme song. Trying to squelch his elation at being part of the World Cup, Ricky went back to work on the album as if nothing had ever happened.

When the strain of making *Vuelve* was finally mitigated, Ricky was faced with choosing a title that would befit the album. Written by Ricky's close friend Franco DeVita, the song ''Vuelve'' made a powerful impact on Ricky. It was a message to those fans who had stuck with him throughout the years. " 'Vuelve' means come back," he interpreted for *Box Talk*. "It's the need for the muse to come back. It's the need for the audience to come back. It's the need to go back to my culture. And it's also a very romantic song. It's a song that is pure Catholic, I must say, for me. This is my life. This is who I am today. This is Ricky Martin."

CHAPTER 8

Drinking From the Cup of Life

In February of 1998, the long-awaited *Vuelve* was distributed to music stores around the world. Ricky speculated about the public's response, wondering if they would appreciate the work he had done. Right before the world was introduced to his latest public offering, the singer issued a statement inviting fans from around the globe to sample the fruits of his labor. "In this project, there is a little piece of each and every one of you," he wrote. "It's a compromise to take our cultures, feelings, and language to the entire world. In actuality, more than sixty-five countries will receive the album on its release date. And we hope that soon there will be more. We are convinced that we have made musical excellence, and we want you to make it yours."

This heartfelt appeal gave Ricky the chance to reach out to his listeners. As he would soon find out, he had many more fans than he'd originally believed. The buying frenzy that followed immediately on the heels of the album's release date was proof of the people's love for Ricky's music. Never had an album of his been snapped up with the voracious alacrity the fans seemed to have reserved for *Vuelve*.

Critics, too, were in raptures over the new CD. Stephen Thomas Erlewine, a music reviewer for *All-Music Guide*, wrote, "*Vuelve* continues the strengths of Ricky Martin's *A Medio Vivir*, offering a good collection of danceable Latin pop and nortenas that are professionally produced and effortlessly catchy." A critic for the *Los Angeles Times* also appreciated the artistry apparent in every song. "A mix of delicate ballads and joyous dance numbers, *Vuelve* belongs to a species that is almost defunct in Latin pop: an album that transcends the year or even the decade in which it was made."

In its first four weeks in the stores, the album established itself as one of the most commercially successful among Latin artists, selling over one million copies in that short breadth of time. It was only a matter of time until that number would soar dramatically, because Ricky's performance at the World Cup '98 was bound to elevate his status as a performer to an even higher plane.

For months before the big event, he was anxious about singing in front of an estimated two billion viewers. The occasion had him turned completely inside out. Many times he questioned his competence and his nerve. "For months I couldn't think of anything but that performance," he explained. "There were times I thought: 'In heaven's name, what am I doing?' I mean, it's the whole world watching. I still can't believe they asked me to do it."

An event of such sweeping proportions required extensive preparations. Ricky even relocated to Paris for a few weeks in order to complete his promotional obligations and ready his band for their moment in the sun—lucky thing too, for Air France pilots would decide to strike mere days before the World Cup festivities got under way.

After just two rehearsals with the official World Cup orchestra, Ricky was ready to sing his heart out. He was so nervous that he decided not to think about the magnitude of his undertaking until it was finally completed. "We knew that millions of fans would be seeing me in their houses," he recalled during an interview with CNN. "That was tremendous, taking into account that we had not had more than two rehearsals with the orchestra. But I decided not to think about any of that until I left the stadium."

Walking up the steps to World Cup stage, Ricky felt like an astronaut about to embark on one of the most exciting missions of his life. With 80,000 people in the stands and billions stationed in front of their televisions worldwide, the performance could be a giant step for Ricky and the Latino community he represented. All of the entertainer's focus went into delivering the best show possible. In fact, Ricky was concentrating so intently that he almost forgot where he was. "When I entered the field, I didn't want to think a lot about it," he informed *El Nuevo Herald*. "If I had started thinking that so many millions of people were watching me, I probably would have gone crazy."

Thoughts of his grandmother, his family, and his heritage raced through Ricky's mind. To ground himself, he tried to focus on those people whom he felt most comfortable with. "I'm just a normal boy from Puerto Rico," he told *Holland*. "Do you know what I kept thinking of during that performance? My grandmother. She was watching me on television in Puerto Rico. She's really very proud of me!"

It wasn't until Ricky left the stage and the dancing spectators that he could finally sort out what had transpired. The notion that people from all around the world were watching didn't occur to him, until, that is, he placed a call to his mother who had been watching at home. "It all hit me when I left the field and called my mother in Puerto Rico to see if the satellite had worked right," he recounted to *El Nuevo Herald*. "I heard my mother, who was crying and was saying, 'You crossed yourself at the same time that I was crossing myself.' That was when I said, 'This really happened.'"

Deliberately blocking out the significance of his performance while he was on stage, Ricky had to battle the nervousness only after he had retired to the calm shelter of his dressing room. It was then that he released all the extreme emotions that went hand in hand with bringing the world to its feet. As soon as he was alone, Ricky's façade crumpled and he cried and shook for what seemed like hours. "It was a little sad, but it was okay," he reported. "You know what? I didn't feel anything while I was on stage. I actually realized what I had just done when I went back into the dressing room. That's when I started shivering. It really was beautiful."

Singing their own song at the World Cup is an honor that only a handful of artists can claim as their own. Ricky's performance of "La Copa de la Vida" clinched the global domination that began only one year earlier. That one performance taught Ricky more than all of his former shows combined. He and the world were truly richer for having had the memory. "It was a fascinating way to exchange cultures," he told *Hey, Hey, It's Saturday*. "There were more than a billion people watching me perform my music. My music is my rhythms, my sound and it's the way I present where I come from. It was fascinating. The audience was very warm. The reactions and comments from the media, internationally speaking, were very positive.

That's the kind of stage I want to go back onto because it's a stage where you grow up as an entertainer and it really was fascinating.''

Better still, the day after Ricky's performance, all of Europe and the Spanish-speaking world was singing and dancing to the beat of his rousing World Cup anthem. The words "Go, Go, Gol! Alé, Alé, Alé!" had transcended the context of soccer and found their way into the discotheques, the radio stations, and the very heart of the international youth culture.

The World Cup achievement established Ricky as one of the most popular entertainers in the world. With sales exceeding 8 million worldwide, *Vuelve* soon skyrocketed to the top of the Billboard Latin 50 chart and even crossed over to the domestic charts. It also became the number two top-selling Latin album for 1998. Ricky was just as surprised as anyone about the global feedback. It seemed that everyone who saw him sing that night wanted to reach out and touch him, to feel what it would be like to be so vital, so optimistic, and full of life.

Besides being named one of *People en Español's* 10 Most Intriguing People of 1998 (along with Antonio Banderas, Jennifer Lopez, Alejandra Guzman, and Adela Noriega), Ricky was the only Hispanic selected to participate in recording Pope Juan Pablo II's album of poems. Other contributors included Luciano Pavarotti, Michael Bolton, and Celine Dion.

Ricky's meeting with the Pope was a thrilling experience. "Look, I was raised in the Catholic religion, but it doesn't matter what your belief is, whatever it might be, you feel like your lungs are going to explode because you immediately fill them with air when you see him," he said. "Meeting him gave me a lot of serenity, a lot of peace. He is like an angel. He swept away a lot of the 'skeptic' that was inside of me. I found in those four letters—Pope—the wondrous thing of simplicity.''

The encounter also allowed Ricky to finally come to grips with a tragedy that had haunted him for years. As a young boy, his faith in God had been tested by the senseless killing of a priest. Ricky had known the priest rather well, and was traumatized by his death. Much of the piousness he had felt as a young boy had died on that day. Nothing less than the Pope's own blessing could wash away the pain and negativity that had tracked the singer ever since the murder of his friend.

''I was an altar boy for many years and I had a painful experience,'' he continued. ''The priest that gave me my first communion was assassinated in the Church and that was very dramatic for me. It is something that I cannot forget. I didn't see it, but it was very shocking, as though this rage invaded me, and I asked myself, 'Why? Such a good person.' And from that time on I would say that nothing mattered to me, and that lasted for a while. Little by little, you feel like you are living in hell, and you say, 'Hold it! Something bad is happening here, let's correct it, let's figure out what is happening, let's make it better.' You have to look for something spiritual.''

Having paddled through some of life's murkier waters, Ricky got the chance to lighten up when fashion guru Georgio Armani asked him to model for his clothing line. At first, Ricky hoped he would get the chance to strut his stuff on the catwalk. But Armani's motives were far loftier.

Ricky's role would not be relegated to a mere runway cameo. He would be the star of the whole show.

His enthusiasm was unmistakable. "I'm certainly going to do that," he effused. "I love fashion and Armani is one of my heroes, so I didn't have to think long before I said yes. It's a great honor for me."

While the singer busied himself with the glamorous world of fashion, *Vuelve*'s sales were growing with each passing day. Although his last tour had ended in exhaustion, Ricky was once again restless and raring to travel the world. Choosing Puerto Rico to open his worldwide trek, he proceeded to travel through Italy, France, Australia, Spain, Germany, Turkey, Chile, and the United States, spreading his message of unity and tolerance.

Even though he received a warm welcome wherever he went, Ricky was especially pleased by the ease with which he was able to penetrate new areas like Portugal. "It was beautiful and now it's wonderful, because Portugal is a very important country to my career," he told *Teenager*. "It's a sincere audience, and the applause is always true. They're people that are always open to other cultures and that pleases me very much. I hope that our relations stay like this, on the right path."

No matter how far his travels took him, Ricky's favorite leg of the voyage was the United States. Like Puerto Rico, the States had seen him through some of his earlier stages of development, and Ricky felt a certain sense of loyalty to the nation that had embraced him as a youth. Knowing that many of his old friends would be watching him from the audience made the experience special.

To Ricky, however, the U.S. represented unconquered territory, the final frontier.

Everywhere he went, he'd become a major star, but the United States presented a formidable challenge. It

was one of the few countries that still looked at Ricky
as a Latin star. His music was in Spanish, and much
like Selena before him, it would take an English album
for Ricky to cross over the barrier separating Latino
music from the Billboard pop charts. But while mainstream American audiences had not been as quick to
come around to his many charms as Puerto Rico or
Europe, Ricky's concerts still managed to draw capacity crowds. The success gave him hope for the future.

After outdoing himself at several sold-out shows in
Los Angeles and Miami, Ricky concluded his American tour at New York's Madison Square Garden in
June, 1998. ''I am anxious, many people would say
nervous, but I prefer to denominate it anxious,'' he explained. ''New York is very special and I wanted to
finish here. The concert is going to be the same one, is
going to be the same passion, the same spirit. They are
going to see many visual effects on stage, they are very
influenced by the theater. The first time that I appeared
in the Madison was in 1988 and ten years later the
dream is occurring once again, but now I'm a solo artist. My life has been cycles of ten years.''

Before heading over to the packed Garden, Ricky
made a promotional appearance at New York City's
Virgin Megastore. The scene was something right out
of Hitchcock's horrifying peckfest, *The Birds*. But instead of our fine feathered friends flocking from every
direction, thousands of screaming fans swarmed the unsuspecting heartthrob right in the middle of Times
Square. When the commotion died down and Ricky
was situated in a chair, a long line had formed as love-
struck and curious Americans tried to get a look at
Ricky. Chatting politely with his admirers all day, he
received thousands of marriage proposals, flowers, and,
of course, Beanie Babies. Ricky's visit to New York

created an immense fracas; a response that would help set the stage for his inevitable English crossover.

The summer of 1998 would be marked as one of the best and worst of Ricky's life. Just as he had finished laying the groundwork for a spectacular future in music, his grandmother passed away. From that point on, life as he'd come to know it was over.

When Ricky first got word of his grandmother's hospitalization, he immediately cancelled his tour and rushed home to Puerto Rico. "The last time that I was there was for a very sad reason," he later lamented to *Bravo*. "My grandmother Iraida was almost dead and I passed eleven days by looking after her at the hospital. It was the most difficult time of my life! My grandmother was seventy-six years old and she has suffered of cancer since forty years old."

The trip took a heavy toll on Ricky's emotional state. Ever since his boyhood, the bond he shared with Iraida went beyond mere words. Her endless supply of unconditional love warmed his heart no matter how far away he may have traveled. He had grown to rely on her for wisdom and guidance, she had meant the world to him, and now, Ricky didn't know how he would fare without her. "She was like my mother to me," he explained. "When I came back to school, it was she that took care of me, because my parents were working. I can't believe that she is not here anymore with us."

Watching his grandmother struggle on her deathbed, Ricky wanted to reach out and help her. Yet there was nothing he or the doctor could do. His grandmother could hardly even recognize him. Paying little attention to his parents' entreaties to get some rest, Ricky would not leave her side. Only when Ricky's song cut through the stillness of her hospital room did Iraida finally release her hold on life and slip peacefully into the next world. "I think that she recognized me, because she smiled to me when I sang one of my songs to her," Ricky described their last moment together. "When she died in my hands, I started to cry."

No matter how hard he tried, he could not get past the loss of his grandmother. Mourning her day and night, he could not reconcile his professional ambitions with this all-consuming tragedy. Instead of finishing his tour, Ricky decided to move back to his house in Miami in order to devote himself to solitude and commemorate his grandmother's memory. Even as his friends and relatives tried to stimulate his interest in his old life, he could not rid himself of feelings of liability and doubt. On some level he felt guilty for not having spent more time with her while she was alive. He blamed his career for taking him away from the one person he loved most.

Strolling along the beach, Ricky tried to sort through his conflicting emotions. He spent his time questioning himself, the meaning of life, and his future. Although he would never have considered it before, the deep depression led him to contemplate retiring from show business altogether. "My grandma died and that disoriented me," he confided in TV Guide. "I thought I was prepared for the moment when she would leave me, but no! It was very painful. So much that I didn't think I could sing and smile on the outside, when I was dying on the inside. Then at that moment, I said to myself, no more! Yes, a month ago I was on the verge of retiring."

Just as Ricky was about to chuck it all—the touring, the recording, the performing—he realized that his grandmother would never have sanctioned the rash decision. Iraida had nurtured Ricky's talent and artistic

ability. Surely, she would not have wanted him to
throw it all away. Sensing her presence by his side and
in his dreams, Ricky knew what he must do.

Giving up all thoughts of early retirement, he returned to music with peace of mind as well as a deeper
understanding of the precious and fragile mystery that
is life. "Now I know that wherever she is, she is in a
better place than we are," he told *TV Guide*. "And I
feel like she communicates with me and it makes me
happy to think that from above she encourages me in
my career and in my mission in my life."

Dedicating the *Vuelve* track "Perdido Sin Ti" to his
grandmother, Ricky had finally come to terms with the
loss. He had suffered, but was stronger for having sur-
vived the ordeal. "I think this song reflects, better than
all songs that I did until today, the sadness of losing
someone that you love," he informed *Bravo*. "That's
the reason why I wanted to dedicate it to my grandmother."

Part of what helped Ricky get through the death of his
grandmother, was his commitment to spreading his music throughout the world. Ever since he had become
popular in Europe, the young performer had been hoping to repeat that success in Asia. With the Chinese,
Koreans, and Japanese all buying up *Vuelve* at breakneck speeds, Ricky seemed to have accomplished exactly that.

Still, he wanted to further secure his position in the
Far East. To ensure success, he would have to travel a
great distance, but he knew that it would be well worth
his time and effort. "Even though I've heard that my
music is listened to in Japan and the Philippines, it's a
must," he told *Estylo*. "Right now I have just confirmed my trip to Japan, the Philippines, and Hong

Kong in April. Let's see what happens. I try to live one day at a time. Tomorrow and yesterday are two eternities that can break you down because they don't exist. Let's just get ready for tomorrow. But Asia is definitely one of my priorities right now."

Visiting Korea, China, the Philippines, Malaysia, and Japan in the deluxe private jet he secured at the bargain price of $700,000, Ricky was glad to find that his concerts brought thousands of gift-bearing fans out of seclusion. Unable to resist Ricky's appeal, each country rolled out a welcome befitting a king. "I'm very happy," he told the *Miami Herald*. "I'm having a great time. Amazing things are happening to me over here. Imagine going to some little town in China and finding all of these Chinese people singing, 'Un, dos, tres, un pasito pa' 'lante, Maria.' I've gotten the Chinese to speak Spanish. Who else can say that?"

What made the tour of Asia especially worthwhile was the time he spent immersed in Eastern cultures and philosophies. Absorbing everything he could during his brief stopover in each country, Ricky hoped that he could one day incorporate his findings into an album. "I want to go and sit on a park bench and go into little restaurants and see how people react, because I need to in order to understand each country better," he reported to the *South China Morning Post*. "There's so much to learn; philosophies, religion, whatever. It doesn't matter what I learn and that I know I will not have the vocabulary to describe it in words. I will keep it to myself and then later I will put it in my music. On my next Spanish album you will hear a lot of Asian influence not only in the music but maybe working with Asian composers too."

While scouring Asia's countryside for inspiration, Ricky's thoughts were drawn closer to home by a calamity that went by the name of Hurricane George. Spreading physical and financial destruction across much of the Caribbean, Puerto Rico, and the Dominican Republic, its 125-mile-per-hour winds and torrential rains brought about damages totaling more than $2.5 billion. News of the devastating disaster caught Ricky completely off guard. With his homeland under peril, he found it difficult to concentrate on his outreach program in Asia.

Although he knew that his nearest and dearest lived out of harm's way, he was anxious to put all of his fears to rest. At length, after several failed telephone connections, he was relieved to find that no one in his family had been hurt by the hurricane. "All my family were so high, so I wasn't too worried," he explained to *Bravo*. "The island was a chaos. There was no electricity and no telephones either. When the highest waves came in my mother was alone at home with a friend."

Knowing that his family was safe was not enough for Ricky. He was concerned about the welfare of his people, and made a generous monetary contribution to the relief efforts. Ricky also took time out of his schedule to appear at the "United for the Caribbean" telethon, which included performances and salutes from such artists as Marc Anthony, Emilio Estefan, Jennifer Lopez, Ruben Blades, Elvis Crespo, Jon Secada, Willy Chirino, Gilberto Santa Rosa, Grupo Mania, and MDO.

With Ricky's influence growing by the day and all his ventures flourishing, he felt that it was time to branch out into something new. Considering his fondness for festivity and good food, Ricky decided to unite his two loves in one special enterprise. He became a restaurateur, opening Casa Salsa on the happening South Beach strip.

In light of Miami's high Latino population and the bustling tourism industry, the idea was as solid as any other Ricky Martin undertaking. Ricky believed that a Puerto Rican restaurant could help to open American eyes to the wealth of his native land's culture. "It is the home of Puerto Rican cooking, where salsa music can be listened and danced to, and where they will be able to taste some of our rums," Jose Benitez, Ricky's partner and co-owner of Casa Salsa, told *El Nuevo Dia*. "It will be a theme restaurant with Puerto Rican cooking where the decoration, as well as the music and the food, will become a representation of Puerto Ricans to the rest of the world."

In order to bring an air of authenticity to the restaurant, Ricky wanted to keep the food faithful to the rich Puerto Rican cooking traditions. He recruited his favorite chef from the Ajilimojili restaurant in Puerto Rico. Soon, they had created a menu featuring some of Ricky's favorite foods; piononos, piñón, carne machada, tostones rellenos, mofongo relleno, asopao, arroz con gandules, pasteles and arañitas, to name but a few. Once all the pieces were in place, Ricky couldn't have been more pleased. Casa Salsa captured the essence of his beloved homeland perfectly.

"When I travel around the world, I miss my island a whole lot, so when the opportunity came to join forces with some other Puerto Rican entrepreneurs to open a restaurant that would, in essence, be a reflection, a re-creation—through its food, its atmosphere, its flavor of what Puerto Rico is and has to offer—I jumped in," Ricky explained. "And when you walk into Casa Salsa, you walk into an environment where you feel like you have walked into a modern Puerto Rican house, offering you one of the best cuisines in all of Latin America.''

With a grand opening slated for December 12, 1998, Casa Salsa was to be one of Ricky's most ambitious and exciting enterprises. The restaurant was situated virtually next door to his friends Emilio and Gloria Estefan's Cuban-themed restaurant. By showcasing memorabilia and offering salsa dance lessons to newcomers, Ricky's gastronomical venture was intended to celebrate his rich heritage. With plans to build Casa Salsas in New York and Los Angeles, Ricky is looking forward to heightening America's awareness of Puerto Rico's many hidden treasures.

CHAPTER 9

Living La Vida Loca

The unprecedented success of the Asian tour meant different things to different people, more money for the record label executives, more promotional opportunities for Ricky's publicist, and more concerts to schedule for his management. For Ricky, however, the warm reception he received in Asia meant that he was ready to take on the formidable challenge of breaking into the American music market.

While some artists consider success in the United States tantamount to "making it," Ricky wasn't looking to prove himself. Gratifying as it would have been to be accepted in the States, he would not let his self-worth be measured by American musical tastes and standards. "Usually people come to the U.S., make it here and then go elsewhere," he explained to *South China Morning Post.* "They think if you don't make it here, you don't make it anywhere. But it is not so in my case. I wanted to work different markets separately on each continent."

Whether it was because he was nervous about releasing his first English album or whether he was concerned about insulting his Spanish-speaking audience, Ricky refused to ascribe too much importance to what would be his fifth album. "Just call it a whim," he told the *Miami Herald*. "If I can make it in Latin America, Europe, and Asia, why wouldn't I want the United States? Well, actually, *General Hospital* did take me to Iowa, and North Dakota too. We still get letters from there. But why not go after that big mainstream success? I don't really need it, no. But why not?"

Never one to run from a challenge, Ricky was goaded into crossing over by the skepticism he encountered. Warned repeatedly about the difficulty of breaking into the U.S. market, he was anxious to dispel the doubts his agenda had inspired. "With my first English record, I swore to myself that I would conquer America," he asserted to *Star Club*. "For that, I have begun a long work process a couple of years ago when I was starring in *General Hospital* . . . People just told me that I wouldn't be able to conquer the United States, but I want to prove them wrong."

Famous first words? Sure, but would Ricky be able to follow them up with artistic greatness?

The singer soon found additional motivation for making his Spanish-English transition. For as long as he could remember, the Latino community had been sorely neglected and misunderstood by the American public. The desire to corrode commonly held stereotypes about Puerto Ricans was what made Ricky attach his name to *General Hospital* and *Les Miserables*, as well as open his new restaurant, Casa Salsa. "It's all about breaking stereotypes," he declared in *Entertainment Weekly*. "For me, the fact that people think Puerto Rico is *Scarface*, that we ride donkeys to school—that has to change."

The professional acclaim that these earlier projects brought, however, was secondary to Ricky's mission of increasing awareness about his culture. The global significance of exposing United States consumers to his brand of Latin pop was not lost on the young performer, who soon finalized his plans for the album. "You can't be mediocre. Look, I could be happy. I could live the rest of my life working in Latin America and that would be fine," he elaborated to *El Norte Newspaper*. "There are many excellent Latin American artists, but there is so much ignorance about the Latin American culture. The ignorance annoys me. You have to go to those countries and begin to remove the stereotypes. And you shouldn't get angry. As I say, it bugs me, but it is just ignorance. I meet people who ask me, 'Where are you from?' I say 'Puerto Rico.' And they say, 'Oh, Costa Rico,' and they associate that with carts and wagons."

Even though he represented only one country, Ricky entered into the arrangement for the English album knowing that he would be speaking for all of Latin America. Seeing himself as a messiah for the entire Latino population, Ricky was eager to create an album that would befittingly represent their principals, ideals, and cultural pride. "My motivation is my people and when I talk about my people, it is all of Latin America," he informed *Latin Style*. "When I talk about Latin America it is a people that for many, many years and many decades were cutting our own wings because we were always hearing that we couldn't do it—we are not able to do it. I just want to go all over the world to let people know that we can do it, that there is talent and hunger for success, that you can count on us."

What previously seemed like a rejection of his heritage had proven to be an affirmation of his loyalty. The English album would not be the departure from his roots that some people considered it to be. In fact, Ricky promised that, as long as he had the chance, he would continue recording in Spanish long after completing the English record. "I think that there is no other language like Spanish," he professed to *Latin Style*. "I think it is the most beautiful language, very romantic. Sometimes you can't quite translate the same emotion or the exact meaning. I won't just stay with English or any other language. I will never stop singing in Spanish—definitely!"

The time was ripe for claiming a place on the American music charts. The year 1999 was pivotal, in that it heralded a new appreciation for Latin music. While Gloria Estefan had been wooing U.S. audiences since the late 1980s, few Latinos were able to maintain that kind of firm grip on the Anglo-centric market. Yet with a Hispanic population in excess of 29 million, the U.S. was primed for a Latin invasion.

Radio stations across Miami and New York are increasingly willing to devote precious air time to Latin music. In some areas, the Spanish television network Telemundo is even more popular than all three of the big networks combined. And with Latin record sales jumping 21 percent in the last year, it seemed that the English debuts of such artists as Ricky Martin, Jennifer Lopez, Shakira, and Marc Anthony could indeed find favor with U.S. audiences. "I have no crystal ball, but my gut tells me that Latin music can be the next big reservoir of talent for mainstream superstars," Sony Music chief Tommy Mottola told *Time* magazine.

Although plenty of Latin artists are willing to claim their place in the English-speaking market, Ricky is the one voted most likely to succeed. With his stunning good looks, catchy rhythms, and electrifying stage presence, he is the star most likely to bridge the language barrier. "Ricky's crossover appeal is endless," said Allison Winkler, director of Latin Events for Nederlander Concerts. ''He has the best potential of any Latin artist for crossover because he has already achieved success in dozens of non-Spanish markets.''

Despite the mountain of praise and support, recording his English-album would not be an easy feat. He no longer had only his own reputation to consider. Millions of people were counting on Ricky to be the next big crossover artist. His first step to crafting a successful album included teaming up with acclaimed producers and friends Emilio Estefan, husband of Gloria Estefan, and Desmond Child, who had produced the hit ''La Copa de La Vida.'' Also contributing songs were Diane Warren, (who has penned songs for Aerosmith, Toni Braxton, Celine Dion, Joe Cocker, Roy Orbison, and LeAnn Rimes), his old friend Robi Rosa, and singer extraordinaire Jon Secada. Because the team was one of the most talented Ricky had ever assembled, he was confident that the album would merit a permanent place in music history.

The magic in the studio was palpable. Everyone believed that they were in the process of creating greatness, a work that would withstand the passage of time. True to form, Ricky demanded as much of himself as ever, if not more. Emilio Estefan described the singer's commitment to excellence to *People En Espanol*: ''He's carrying Latin music throughout the world, and that, to me, since I know how difficult it is to break down barriers, makes me feel proud. He deserves everything he has for his sacrifices.''

Due to unforeseen circumstances, the album was delayed. Working harder than he ever had, Ricky insisted on nothing short of musical perfection, and tried to make up for lost time. ''I'm really late in my album process. And it makes me very anxious,'' he told *Star*

Club. "I'm still working on it in Miami because I want it to be perfect. It's a matter of life and death! Everyone in America is waiting for it. I'm not allowed to make mistakes. I rewrote some texts a million times, I worked my English accent with a teacher."

What made the production of his fifth album especially difficult and time consuming was Ricky's desire to unite Latin and English influences into one seamless musical composition. Unwilling to abandon his signature sound for the American public, he found a way to incorporate the music that inspired him to perform. "The new record will be in English, but it will still have Latin rhythms, the Caribbean mixed with other Latin American influences," he reported to *The Miami Herald.* "There will still be Spanish phrases sprinkled throughout. I think it's my responsibility to take my culture to new places."

With the popularity of artists such as Wyclef Jean, and even songs such as the Macarena, Ricky's goal to retain his many original influences was nothing if not commercially sound. American citizens were slowly opening their ears and hearts to exotic cultures, and Ricky hoped to prove the value of multiculturalism once and for all.

As he was putting the finishing touches on the as-yet-untitled English album, he was honored with one of the most prestigious award nominations in the music industry. On January 27, 1999, Ricky learned that *Vuelve* was one of the contenders vying for the 1999 Grammys' "Best Latin Pop Performance" award!

The accolade had come right out of the clear blue. Ricky had been concentrating so intently on recording his fifth album that he had completely forgotten about the Grammys. When news of his nomination broke, he called his parents to share the joy. Both were just as excited as their son, assuring him that he was a shoo-in for the coveted award.

Because it was his first nomination as a solo artist, Ricky was elated with the prospect of attending the biggest music awards ceremony in the entire world. But when the National Academy of Recording Arts and Sciences (NARAS) called his manager Angelo Medina to request that Ricky perform, his enthusiasm went through the roof. With over 50 million people watching the award show, he would finally get the chance to sing in front of his largest American audience to date. This was just the commercial boost his English album needed to get off the ground. "We are delighted to have such a talented performer on the Forty-first Annual Grammy Awards," commented Michael Greene, President/CEO of NARAS. "As both an actor and performer, he brings a special energy to the show. We are also committed to represent more Latin music in our future endeavors."

Having the opportunity to expose people from all backgrounds to his music, and perform alongside a veritable who's who of legendary U.S. performers—including Madonna, Shania Twain, and Lauryn Hill—was extremely gratifying. Expressing Ricky's sentiment was his manager, Angelo Medina. "For Ricky Martin it is a commitment and another opportunity to continue promoting our culture," he said.

Although Ricky had showcased his talents to billions at the World Cup, he had never before performed in front of such a large, predominantly American audience. Ricky began making preparations for the performance long before the ceremony aired. He was determined to milk this chance for all it was worth. It was a make-it-or-break-it moment. So much was riding on this one performance. If the audience hated him, it meant that his album would suffer from a similar fate. But if they loved him, he could rest assured that they would embrace his first English-language CD in much the same way.

Unlike the rest of the nominees, for Ricky, the award ceremony wasn't about securing a Grammy to display on his mantle, it was about winning over a nation. The pressure to rise to the challenge was considerable, and the singer used every spare moment to stage the type of spectacle American audiences would not soon forget.

On February 24, 1999, Ricky accomplished the impossible. After sitting through performances from some of music's biggest names, the singer took the stage and showed America what making music and performing was all about. Dressed in sleek leather black pants and a tight-fitting, ribbed gray shirt, Ricky looked GQ perfect. But good looks alone would not get him far with this jaded group, who had seemed ambivalent about every live performance preceding his. As winning over this tough crowd seemed unlikely, Ricky jumped on the stage knowing he had nothing to lose. The audience, which had been dangerously close to the brink of boredom, was now alert, happy, and visibly moved.

With a live band stomping through the aisles, streamers flowing through the air, and lights dazzling the viewers from every direction, Ricky's "La Copa De La Vida" had the previously lethargic and critical audience on the edge of their seats. Never before had a new artist had this type of effect at the Grammys. Typically, the reticent crowd reserves standing ovations for special award recipients who are industry veterans. But never, let's repeat, never have Grammy attendants been so accepting, so downright enamored of a new artist. Rosie O'Donnell, the host, summed it up best when she said, "I never heard of him before tonight, but I'm enjoying him so-o-o much."

Ricky was carried away by the commotion he himself was responsible for generating. He had seen the audience clap politely for some of his role models, and hoped that he would at least merit a similar civility. The reality, however, was far more exhilarating. "I guess with all those drums and passion that was flowing onstage, it made everybody dance," he told *USA Today*. "To get the acceptance of an audience is fascinating."

Filled with some of the music industry's most prestigious names, the Shrine Auditorium was like a monument to the best and brightest of the industry. To think that all his favorite singers, musicians, producers, and composers had paid him such a tribute was simply beyond his comprehension. "To see Will Smith doing the jiggy with my song! It's overwhelming."

But the fun wouldn't stop there. After receiving the immense gratification of winning the entire North American continent over with one shake of his hips, Ricky's show-stopping presentation of "La Copa De La Vida" was announced as the winner of a Grammy for "Best Latin Pop Performance." Waving his heavy award in the air, Ricky was beaming as he thanked the NARAS for their recognition. This was truly his night to shine. "The acceptance of the audience is important, but the acceptance of the industry, it means a lot to any artist," Ricky reported backstage to MTV. "This is the beginning. Let's see what happens. I'm taking it one day at a time and all I wanna do is music with quality and do it right."

* * *

Ricky couldn't have asked for a better introduction to the American public. The day after he won the Grammy, record stores in New York, Los Angeles, Miami, and even Utah reported a mass consumption of Ricky's *Vuelve*, with sales of the album rising an astounding 470 percent all over the country. An employee of Salt Lake City's Media Play told *USA Today*, ''We sold out our entire shipment.'' A worker at Tower Records in Los Angeles confirmed the report, ''Women saw how good-looking he was, and that translated to record sales . . . always does.''

Album sales of Ricky's *Vuelve* had never been better in the U.S. But America's adulation and a Grammy would not be the last of his just deserts. Only a week after the ceremony, Ricky was contacted by Madonna, one of his favorite performers. It seems that the two had gotten chummy waiting behind-the-scenes at the Grammys. But, as usual, Madonna wanted more than just friendship. She wanted to collaborate with Ricky on a duet for his new album. Like everyone else who had seen him perform on that magical night, Madonna fell head over heels for the Latin lothario.

The respect and honor between the unlikely pair wasn't one-sided. Ever since he was a teenage boy, Ricky felt a special fondness for the immortal Material Girl. ''After the Grammys, there was like a click between us,'' he expressed to *USA Today*. ''She's so into a changing culture, she always has been. She enjoys the Latin sounds, she's energetic, I'm energetic, so let's do something!''

And do something they did. In March of 1999, the daring duo got together in Los Angeles to discuss plans for a single. The song was envisioned as a blend of each singer's unique style and sound. With Madonna's *Ray of Light* producer William Orbit at the helm and no preconceived expectations on either side, Ricky was confident the collaboration would produce outstanding results. "The way we started, I promised Madonna that if it works for my album, great, if it works for yours, great, for a soundtrack, great, or just to have fun—great," he noted. "Let's not be dealing with a deadline ... let's take it easy. It has to come out of comfort. She doesn't want to sound like me, I don't want to sound like her—it's fusion."

Neither was Madonna the only heavyweight to approach Ricky after his awe-inspiring Grammy debut. Sony CEO Tommy Mottola and Columbia Records President Don Lenner were ready to jump on the singing sensation's bandwagon as well. Although Ricky had long been a key player for Sony's Latin music division, he was now being courted by Sony's mammoth Columbia Records label. The rise in his status had happened overnight, but Ricky didn't seem at all surprised. After agreeing to release *Ricky Martin* on Columbia, he told *Entertainment Weekly* "I knew they'd come to me someday. After the Grammys, it was 'Yo, this is mine!' "

The participation of Sony and Columbia brought a great influx of promotional dollars. Ricky's music videos and public relations campaign were guaranteed to be the best that money could buy, and success seemed inevitable. Of course, nothing is perfect.

The pressure that the music conglomerate put on Ricky to produce, and fast, was just the sort of thorn that could ruin a rosy business arrangement. Specifically, Tommy Mottola's none-too-gentle nudges were almost responsible for tearing apart all of Ricky's and Madonna's plans for a duet. Reportedly, Madonna stomped off the premises, unwilling to heed Mottola's prodding. Ricky couldn't believe it. At length, he convinced the diva to stay the course. "Forget about Clinton," Ricky later remarked, "*that* was politics."

After wrapping the production of the single, both parties agreed that it was good enough to go on Ricky's English album. The duet was the final master stroke, but it was only one of many pièces de résistance that comprised *Ricky Martin*. Contrary to all predictions, America had been very good to Ricky thus far. All that was left to do now was to anxiously await the verdict on the crossover album, and hope that the good fortune would continue to flow uninterrupted.

The pins and needles Ricky had been sitting on for months were about to vanish. The first single, "Living La Vida Loca," off his fifth album was unveiled to the world in the form of a seductive new video. From MTV to VH-1 to The Box, no music network could resist pouncing upon this latest offering. Filled with steamy scenes of Ricky cavorting with a beautiful woman, the video also featured him singing in a salsa dance club. As Ricky shakes his moneymaker on the stage, the story of his tempestuous love affair unfolds through interspersed clips.

A regular feature on *MTV's Total Request Live*, the video was the perfect vehicle for Ricky's transition into English-speaking territories. Duly pleased with the results, Ricky couldn't resist plugging the visual extravaganza. "You have to see it twice! It's a lot of information. It goes from a club to a funky, cheap hotel, to walking in the middle of the city, with lots of dancers, lots of stunts, car crashing."

With the video catching on all over the U.S., plans to release the single were accelerated. Originally produced by the Trackmasters, who have arranged albums for such artists as LL Cool J, Foxy Brown, Nas, and

Mary J. Blige, "Living La Vida Loca" describes women who live dangerously close to the edge, and the effect they have on men. The sound is a curious combination of Latin pop, Euro dance, and the big band sound of swing. The overall effect proved so successful that it drove Ricky back to the studio where he recorded a club remix. With the aid of rappers Big Punisher, Fat Joe, and Cuban Link, Ricky was able to add even more potency to the already spellbinding track.

The first single was a instant crowd pleaser. While it's Ricky's belief that the video should be seen twice for maximum enjoyment, one screening is all it takes to get hooked good and proper. Ricky's unbridled passion for music, dance and *les affairs de coeur* is so potent that it can overwhelm even the staunchest of Goth's true believers, the most militant of hip-hop's emcee wannabes, and the angriest of heavy metal's mosh pit thrashers.

A music reviewer for *Billboard* elaborated on the song's effect. "It's so electrifying, so terrifically filled with life, that even folks at the retirement home down the street could get their groove on with a couple spins. Manic horns and groovy elements à la the music from *Pulp Fiction* define the basic structure of this frantically paced, dance-ready track, while Martin sings his heart out with more enthusiasm than a Broadway diva. Utterly irresistible. This is going to explode."

Although originally about a woman, "Living La Vida Loca" would become Ricky's motto for the year of 1999. His was indeed a crazy life. In one year, he had accomplished what it takes most singers a lifetime to achieve. And who could blame him for working so hard to ingratiate himself into the world's good graces? Ricky relentless ascension to the ranks of international superstardom is a result of being able to do many things extraordinarily well.

Despite his youth, he has never lost sight of his primary mission. As one of today's most prominent proponents of Latin American music and traditions, Ricky is happily saddled with the obligation of bridging the cultural gaps that have shrouded his heritage in a cloak of ignorance. "If I leave my music at this moment, it could destroy something historical for Latin Americans," he professed to *Diversion*. "I do not want them to say that the Latinos came and went away. I must seize the moment."

From performing with Menudo to acting on Broadway to earning his stripes as a solo artist, Ricky is one man who truly transcends the label of pop icon. Blessed with a natural grace, talent, and intelligence, the versatile performer makes the most difficult tasks seem effortless. And while determination and perseverance are all well and good, the ability to actualize the most unattainable goals time and again comes from a place deep within the heart. Above all, Ricky Martin's spiritualism and humility have given him the strength to overcome the skepticism, negativity, and obstacles that were presumed to be his birthrights. Armed with the courage of his convictions and the pride of his Puerto Rican ancestry, Ricky Martin has only begun to show what he and his people are capable of.